WITHDRAWN

DEC -- 2012

DATE DUE

KNITTING SWEATERS FROM AROUND THE WORLD

18 HEIRLOOM PATTERNS
IN A VARIETY OF STYLES AND TECHNIQUES

Kari Cornell, Editor

Voyageur Press

First published in 2012 by Voyageur Press, an imprint of MBI Publishing Company, 400 First Avenue North, Suite 300, Minneapolis, MN 55401 USA

Voyageur Press titles are also available at discounts in bulk quantity for industrial or sales-promotional use. For details write to Special Sales Manager at MBI Publishing Company, 400 First Avenue North, Suite 300, Minneapolis, MN 55401 USA.

To find out more about our books, visit us online at www.voyageurpress.com.

ISBN-13: 978-0-7603-4265-7

Printed in China

Editor: Kari Cornell
Design Manager: James Kegley
Layout: Mandy Kimlinger
Photography: rau+barber
Stylist: Libby Fransen
Hair and makeup: Angelia

Front and back cover: Photography by rau+barber
Page 11: vintage postcard, *Voyageur Press Archives*
Page 49: vintage postcard, *Voyageur Press Archives*
Page 69: Domestic thrift—A study from real life—Ireland, by Charleton H., c. 1904, *Library of Congress Prints and Photographs Division, #LC-USZ62-123755*
Page 99: vintage postcard, *Voyageur Press Archives*
Page 119: Navajo woman, holding yarn, c. 1904. 120925, *Library of Congress, Prints and Photographs Division, #LC-USZ62-120925*

Library of Congress Cataloging-in-Publication Data

Knitting sweaters from around the world : heirloom patterns in a variety of styles and techniques / Kari Cornell, editor.
    pages cm
Includes bibliographical references and index.
 Summary: "Knitting Sweaters from Around the World brings together a sampling of patterns from Scandinavia, Europe, the United Kingdom, Ireland, the East, and the West, featuring creative works from well-known designers"--Provided by publisher.
 ISBN 978-0-7603-4265-7 (alk. paper)
 1. Knitting--Patterns. 2. Sweaters. I. Cornell, Kari A.
 TT825.K66 2012
 746.43'2--dc23
                    2012005912

ACKNOWLEDGMENTS

A book of this sort is an ambitious endeavor, and it wouldn't have been possible without the hard work and creative know-how of many talented designers. A big thank-you to Dawn Brocco, Beth Brown-Reinsel, Donna Druchunas, Candace Eisner Strick, Sue Flanders, Gretchen Funk, Kate Larson, Melissa Leapman, Cynthia LeCount Samaké, Hélène Magnússon, Heather Ordover, Kristin Spurkland, and Pinpilan Wangsai. I'm thrilled with the variety of fun patterns in this collection, and I feel honored to have had the opportunity to work with each contributor. Kudos go to Donna Druchunas for once again digging into the enticing history of knitting to write a most interesting introduction to the book. I'm grateful to Rita Greenfeder for her technical editing expertise. A big thank-you to rau+barber for the top notch photography, to stylist Libby Fransen for her keen eye for detail, and to hair and makeup artist Angelia for making the models look great. Thanks to Becky Pagel, James Kegley, Mandy Kimlinger, and the rest of the design team for all that they do to make Voyageur Press books look their best.

CONTENTS

INTRODUCTION

By Donna Druchunas

Although legend has it that Jesus wore a seamless sweater knitted in-the-round, in reality, knitting was not invented until several centuries later. Originally used to make socks, mittens, hats, and many other small projects, knitting was first used to make the various styles of shirts worn as outerwear that we know of as sweaters today sometime between the seventeenth and nineteenth century.

Knitters made shirts as early as the fourteenth century, but these were worn as undergarments. Even the blue silk shirt knitted in an allover knit-and-purl pattern at a gauge of 22 stitches per inch (yes, per inch, not per 4 inches!) worn by England's King Charles I when he was executed in 1649 was likely made to be worn as an undershirt.

Danish blouses with knit-and-purl patterning were the first sweaters made to be worn as outer garments. Woolen nightshirts called *nattrøjer* were commonly worn by people of all classes for centuries. Those who could not afford two separate garments wore a vest or bodice over the knitted shirt during the day. The earliest *nattrøjer* were worn by both men and women. Over time, men stopped wearing them, and the *nattrøjer* evolved into a short, body-hugging style that accentuated a woman's figure and complemented the traditional Danish woman's costume.

The word "sweater" was coined in the nineteenth century by British sportsmen who wore the knitted garments while riding horses and rowing. Before that, sweaters were known as jumpers, jerseys, or frocks. Today, the word "jumper" is still used to refer to a knitted pullover in most of the English-speaking world.

One of the first cardigans, defined as knitted jackets that open in the front and are normally secured with buttons, was made in Germany and worn by Count Palatine Ottheinrich, who died in 1559. The word "cardigan," however, refers to the 7th Earl of Cardigan, James Thomas Brudenell, who wore a knitted jacket during the Crimean War in the 1800s and is credited with making the style famous.

These earliest sweaters were knitted in-the-round, on multiple double-pointed needles, producing seamless garments that were custom made to fit the wearer. Sweaters made with multiple colors, such as Norwegian pullovers, were usually knit as plain tubes and cut open to create neck and armhole openings, while others made with single-color texture patterns, such as British fishermen's ganseys, were shaped as they were knitted.

Later, most often when garments were being made specifically for sale or publication, traditional designs, like Aran cable sweaters, were knit flat rather than in-the-round to make it easier for production knitting and to create multiple sizes. In the nineteenth and twentieth centuries, dressmaking techniques were often used in sweater design; sweaters were knitted in flat pieces and sewn together to allow for more complicated shaping and a more contemporary and stylish fit.

Some of the designs in this book, like the Cowichan-Inspired Swallows & Ivy Wrap Cardigan on page 120, the St. Olaf Men's Fair Isle pullover on page 70, and the Eriskay Gansey on page 88 are very traditional garments, allowing you to try the same stitches and techniques used by the knitters who invented these designs. Other sweaters, such as the Bulgarian Roses Intarsia Cardigan on page 62 and the Turkish Delight Sweater on page 100, were inspired by patterns and stitches used on accessories in a particular country or region. And some sweaters, like the Japanese Kimono on page 112, which was adapted from traditional woven clothing, or the Kinloch Aran Pullover on page 82, which is an updated version of an early-twentieth-century idea, are modern knitting designs.

I hope that as you browse through these pages, you'll be inspired by the many wonderful sweater designs in this book. Select one or two, pick up your yarn and needles, cast on, and celebrate the accomplishments of knitters from around the world.

Albanian girls gather to knit, c. 1923. Frank and Frances Carpenter Collection, Library of Congress Prints and Photographs Division #LC-USZ62-106363

SWEATERS OF SCANDINAVIA

FINNISH SWEATER: PÄIVÄTÄR

DESIGN BY HEATHER ORDOVER

A general search for "Finnish sweaters" will reveal a single example: the Korsnäs. This is *the* traditional Finnish winter garment, and it combines knit and crochet in striking ways—the lower, strong edge; the shoulders, strengthened against stretching; the cuffs, which will never wear out. The Korsnäs pattern is available in many forms online and recently in magazine form, but a slightly shaped cardigan version is not. Using traditional Finnish patterning, this sweater brings together the old and the new. ❧

Sizes
Adult Small (Medium, **Large**, XLarge, XXLarge)

Finished Measurements
Chest: 34 (38, **42**, 46, 52)"/86.5 (96.5, 106.5, 117, 132)cm
Front Length: 21 (22, 23, 24, 25)"/53.5 (56.5, 58.5, 61, 63.5)cm
Back Length: 23 (24, 25, 26, 27)"/58.5 (61, 63.5, 66, 68.5)cm

Materials ❹
- Berroco *Ultra Alpaca*, 50% Alpaca/50% wool, 100g/3.5oz, 215yds/198m per skein: Masa #6225 (MC), 2 (2, 3, 3, 3) skeins; Redwood Mix #6281 (A) and Pea Soup Mix #6276 (B), 2 (2, 2, 2, 2) skeins each; Oceanic #0442 (C), 1 skein
- Size 8 (5mm) 40"/101.5cm long circular needle (or two shorter circular needles, one for front, one for back, to knit in-the-round) or size needed to obtain gauge
- Size 8 (5mm) double-pointed needles
- Size 6 (4.25mm) 60"/152.5cm long circular needle for button band
- Size E/4 (3.5mm) crochet hook
- Stitch markers
- Waste yarn or stitch holder
- Nine 3/4"/2cm diameter buttons (front band)
- Four 1/2"/1.25cm diameter buttons (cuffs)
- Tapestry needle

Gauge
20 sts and 26 rows in 4"/10cm in St st on size 8 (5mm) needles for size Large.
Adjust needle size as necessary to obtain correct gauge.

PATTERN NOTE

Sizes: Because the lower and upper edges are complete patterns, this sweater has been designed for size Large. The *easiest* adjustment for other sizes is to change needle size to obtain a different gauge. A smaller needle size (and/or different yarn) with different tension results will result a smaller sweater.

For example:

- At 5 sts to the inch on size 8 (5mm) needle, the chest will be 42"/106.5cm (size Large as written) with a CYCA #4 (8WPI) yarn.

- At 5.5 sts to the inch on size 7 needle, the chest will be 38"/96.5cm (size Medium).

- At 6 sts to the inch on size 6 needle, the chest will be 34"/86.5cm (size Small).

If you go up a needle size and/or up a yarn size (CYCA #5):

- At 4.5 sts to the inch on size 9 needle, the chest will be 46"/117cm (XLarge).

- At 4 sts to the inch on size 10 needle, the chest will be 52"/132cm (XXLarge).

- Carry the yarn loosely while doing colorwork. Carrying the yarn too tightly in some places and too loosely in others will make the fabric pucker. You can always tighten a stitch later. You can't do anything to rescue a too-tight patch of colorwork.

- The body of the sweater is knit in-the-round from bottom edge to top with a provisional cast on and steeks. There are many ways to steek successfully both with and without sewing machines. The sleeves of the sample sweater were steeked using hand basting and the crochet method. The central steek used a sewing machine. Steeks in this pattern include instructions for placket closure.

- A provisional cast on is used to make pickup for the linen stitch edging easier.

- The sleeves are knit from the shoulder to the cuff. You will pick up stitches at the edge of the steek and knit toward the cuff. Using the smaller needle for the pickup round will help ensure a neat armhole.

- The back of the neck includes short rows for fit. These can be eliminated if desired. End with Round 52 of Chart C, omitting the final motif.

INSTRUCTIONS

Body

With A and larger circular needle, using provisional cast-on, CO 208 sts as foll:

CO 6 steek sts, pm, CO 52 for right front, pm, CO 104 for back, pm, CO 52 for left front, pm, CO 6 steek sts, place colored marker for beg of rnd—208 sts + 12 steek sts.

Rnd 1: With A, k6 for steek, sm, k52 for right front, sm, k104 for back, sm, k52 for left front, sm, k6 for steek.

Rnds 2–3: Knit, slipping all markers.

Shaping

Note: Beg decs on Rnd 18 for waist shaping (indicated on chart).

Dec 1 st before and after each side marker, every 2nd rnd once. Dec 1 st before and after each side marker every 4th rnd 7 times—176 sts.

Note: Beg incs on Rnd 48.

Inc 1 st before and after each side marker every 4th rnd 8 times—208 body sts + 12 steek sts.

Complete Chart A, then cont to Chart B (Front Right).

Note: Chart B includes the upper body patterning and contains indications for the armhole steeks and neck shaping.

Armhole Steeks

On Rnd 33 of Chart B, work to first side marker, sm, CO 7 steek sts, pm, work to next side marker, CO 7 steek sts, pm, knit to end of rnd.

Neck Shaping

On next rnd, beg by binding off steek, then with different yarn CO 8 sts for neck shaping, cont in pat around, BO last 8 sts, change yarn and BO rem steek, CO 3 neck steek sts, pm for beg of rnd.

On Rnd 35, CO 4 neck steek sts, pm, and cont pat—177 sts total (170 body sts + 7 sts for new neck steek).

Cont in pat foll Front Right, Upper Edge Back, and Front Left Charts B, C, and D; at the same time, shaping neck as foll:

Dec rnds: At start of all dec rnds, knit steek sts, sm, dec 1 (ssk), knit around in pat to 2nd neck steek marker, dec 1 st (k2tog) working dec rnd every other rnd 8 times (see Left and Right Front Charts B and D).

Cont in rnds foll charts until piece measures 21 (22, 23, 24, 25)"/53.5 (56.5, 58.5, 61, 63.5)cm for Left and Right Fronts and 23 (24, 25, 26, 27)"/58.5 (61, 63.5, 66, 68.5)cm from top of Back to bottom edge (Rnd 118).

BO all sections and steeks separately (front, neck, 2 armhole steeks). BO each set of shoulder sts (34 sts for each shoulder, front and both sides of back), BO 36 center back neck sts or leave center back sts on waste yarn to seamlessly pick up for band.

Seam Shoulders

Machine stitch main center and neck steeks and cut sweater front open through the center of the steeks.

Note: It is not suggested to use Kitchener st to join shoulder sts, as the weight of the sweater would put too much stress on that join. BO and seam the shoulders.

Create Steek Placket

Starting at the lower corner with RS facing, use a crochet hook to pick up in the space where the sts change from steek to pat on right front. Pick up evenly, 1 st for each row. Place each picked-up st onto smaller needle. Purl back so that purl sts will be hidden and knit sts will be visible on the inside of the sweater, covering the steek.

Cont in St st for 1"/2.5cm or length needed to cover cut steek when folded to the inside of the sweater. Change to main body color for 2 rows, ending on purl row, leaving a tail 3 times the length of the placket (approx 60"/152.5cm). Lightly steam placket into place, then thread tail through a yarn needle and gently "Kitchener" sts off needle, duplicate stitching loosely to body sts. If the placket is pulled too tightly, it will pull on the body sts and be obvious when worn. Rep for left side and right and left neck steeks.

Sleeves

Without cutting steeks: With B and crochet hook, work in the gap between steek sts and pat sts, placing picked-up sts onto dpns as foll: 43 sts along back, 2 sts for shoulder, pm, 1 more st for shoulder, 43 sts along front and 5 sts at underarm, pm for beg of rnd—94 sts.

Note: Once sleeve sts have been picked up and 5–10 rnds have been completed, you may secure and cut the steek. The sample was steeked using the crochet method. Elizabeth Zimmermann's herringbone stitch was used with gentle application of an iron set to steam in order to press steeks toward the sleeve, then attached. As before, stitch the steek loosely to the sleeve using a complementary color.

Decs (indicated on each side of center line on chart):

Rnds 1–3: Knit around in B.

Even Rnds 4–18: K1, k2tog, knit to within 2 sts from marker, ssk.

Odd Rnds 5–17: Knit even.

Cont dec every 4th rnd once, every 8th rnd 3 times, then every 4th rnd 4 times. Cont in pat st until sleeve measures 15"/38cm, ending on Rnd 73.

Place sleeve sts on a holder or scrap yarn, keeping markers in place or replacing with safety pins.

Complete 2nd sleeve.

Edging

Using smaller 60"/152.5cm long needle, start at lower right corner, with A and crochet hook, to pick up sts through front pat st and placket evenly for the first 6 rows, then skipping every 3rd st until the last 6 rows, which should be picked up evenly (80 sts picked up for right front); pm, pick up 8 sts across right-side bound-off neck shaping sts, pm, pick up 17 sts evenly through right neck steek placket and pat sts as for front right side, pm; knit across 36 back sts if left live or pick up 36 sts across back if they were bound off, pm; pick up 17 sts evenly through left neck steek placket and pat sts, pm, pick up 8 sts across left-side bound-off neck shaping sts, pm, pick up sts through front pat st and placket evenly for the first 6 rows, then skipping every 3rd st until the last 6 rows, which should be picked up evenly (80 sts picked up for left front), pm. Remove sts from provisional cast-on as you knit them—454 sts. Sl last st onto the left needle and slip 2nd st over first and off—453 sts. Pm for beg of rnd.

Beg Linen St

Rnd 1: (K1, sl 1 wyif) around; end with k1, sm.

Rnd 2: (Sl 1 wyif, k1) around; end with sl 1 wyif, sm.

Rnds 3–5: Rep Rnds 1–2 once more, then Rnd 1 once.

Rnds 6–19: Foll Chart F, rep buttonholes as indicated on chart 9 times. **Note:** If it is too difficult to put in the final buttonhole—indicated in pat by the blue box—while knitting in pat, it can be duplicate stitched in later, making the buttonhole carefully by basting around the indicated sts quite tightly, then delicately cutting the center sts.

Rnd 20: BO.

Sew buttons to left front edging.

Cuffs

Note: With careful positioning, these can be made two at a time on two circular needles or with magic loop. Beg by laying the sweater buttoned up, face down. Using locking stitch markers or safety pins, mark the top of each sleeve (should line up roughly with shoulder seam) and the bottom of each sleeve (should line up roughly with underarm seam).

Count up 10 sts from bottom of each sleeve. Mark these sts with unique markers. This will indicate the opening for the cuff.

Set-up

Beg at colored marker, slip sts from waste yarn or holders onto the smaller needle. Using cable cast-on, CO 5 sts at beg of rnd, knit to colored marker, CO 5 sts. Turn, purl to end.

Beg Linen St

RS: (K1, sl 1 wyif) across, end k2.

WS: (P1, sl 1 wyib) across, end p2.

Cont in pat for 2"/5cm (or to desired length), then beg Chart G, placing 6 reps evenly starting after 6th st on a knit side. As on button band, do not sl 1 wyif over the motif.

BO. Sew buttons to close cuffs (no buttonholes).

Finishing

Weave in ends. Block lightly with steam.

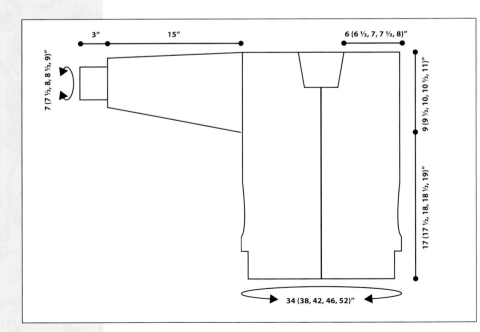

Chart A

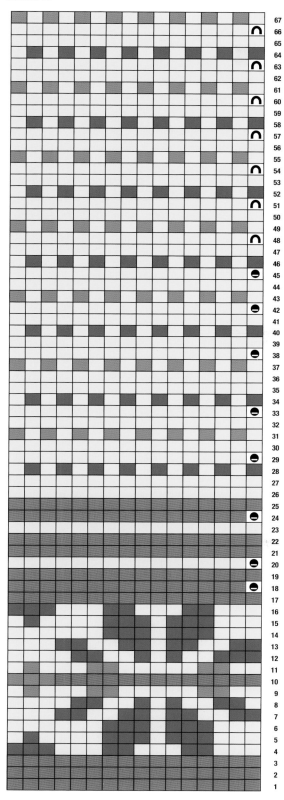

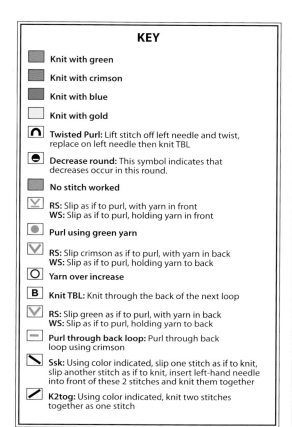

KEY

Knit with green

Knit with crimson

Knit with blue

Knit with gold

Twisted Purl: Lift stitch off left needle and twist, replace on left needle then knit TBL

Decrease round: This symbol indicates that decreases occur in this round.

No stitch worked

RS: Slip as if to purl, with yarn in front
WS: Slip as if to purl, holding yarn in front

Purl using green yarn

RS: Slip crimson as if to purl, with yarn in back
WS: Slip as if to purl, holding yarn to back

Yarn over increase

B **Knit TBL:** Knit through the back of the next loop

RS: Slip green as if to purl, with yarn in back
WS: Slip as if to purl, holding yarn to back

Purl through back loop: Purl through back loop using crimson

Ssk: Using color indicated, slip one stitch as if to knit, slip another stitch as if to knit, insert left-hand needle into front of these 2 stitches and knit them together

K2tog: Using color indicated, knit two stitches together as one stitch

Chart B

Chart C

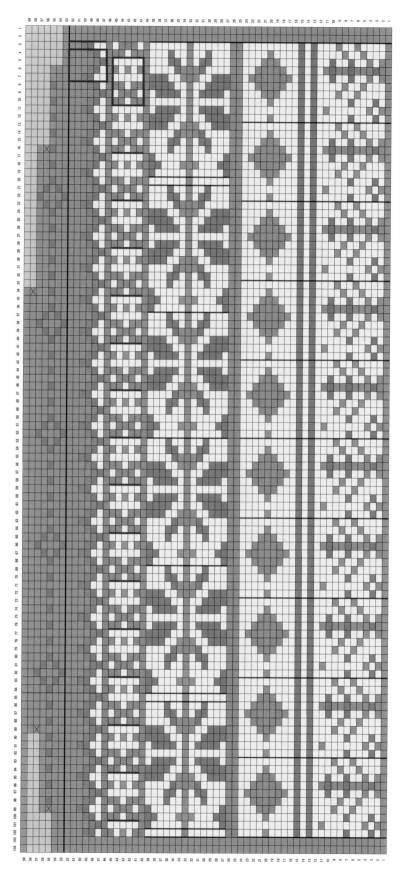

Chart G

Chart D

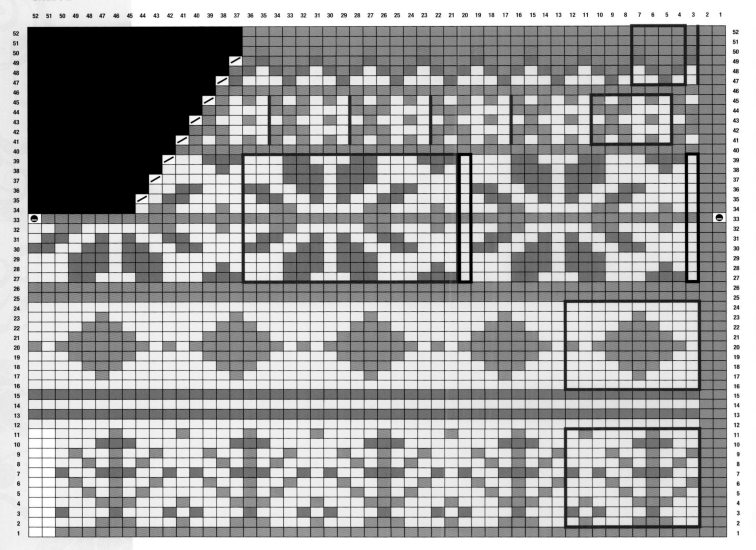

KEY

⬛	Knit with green
⬛	Knit with crimson
⬛	Knit with blue
⬜	Knit with gold
⋒	**Twisted Purl:** Lift stitch off left needle and twist, replace on left needle then knit TBL
⬤	**Decrease round:** This symbol indicates that decreases occur in this round.
▨	**No stitch worked**
⍛	**RS:** Slip as if to purl, with yarn in front **WS:** Slip as if to purl, holding yarn in front
⊙	**Purl using green yarn**
⍌	**RS:** Slip crimson as if to purl, with yarn in back **WS:** Slip as if to purl, holding yarn to back
O	**Yarn over increase**
B	**Knit TBL:** Knit through the back of the next loop
⍌	**RS:** Slip green as if to purl, with yarn in back **WS:** Slip as if to purl, holding yarn to back
−	**Purl through back loop:** Purl through back loop using crimson
◥	**Ssk:** Using color indicated, slip one stitch as if to knit, slip another stitch as if to knit, insert left-hand needle into front of these 2 stitches and knit them together
◢	**K2tog:** Using color indicated, knit two stitches together as one stitch

Chart E

Columns: 25 24 23 22 21 20 19 18 17 16 15 14 13 12 11 10 9 8 7 6 5 4 3 2 1

Rows: 73 down to 1

Chart F

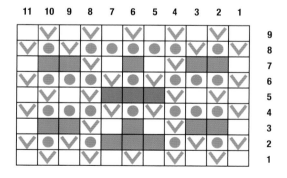

Columns: 11 10 9 8 7 6 5 4 3 2 1

Rows: 9 8 7 6 5 4 3 2 1

ICELANDIC YOKE CARDIGAN

DESIGN BY GRETCHEN FUNK

This sweater is my homage to the original *lopapeysas*. The *lopapeysas*, or Icelandic yoke sweater, has a fairly recent history despite its traditional look. The striking yoke patterns, which decrease from the shoulders to the neck, create a knit necklace of geometric shapes. Wool from the Icelandic sheep has long fibers, making it cozy and strong, and the best insulation for harsh conditions. The Léttlopi yarn from Westminster Fibers is made in Iceland, making it the perfect choice. The added option of a cardigan or pullover can fit a knitter's personal style. ❧

Sizes
Adult Small (Medium, **Large**, XLarge, XXLarge)

Finished Measurements
Cardigan style (1"/2.5cm of ease from button band):
Chest: 37 (39, **42**, 45, 49)"/94 (99, 106.5, 114.5, 124.5)cm
Length: 24.5 (26.5, 27.5, 29, 30)"/62 (67.5, 70, 73.5, 76)cm

Materials 〔4〕
- Léttlopi (Lite-Lopi) distributed by Westminster Fibers,100% wool, 50g/1.75oz, 109yds/100m per skein: Oatmeal #85 (MC), 7 (7, 8, 8, 10) skeins; Blacksheep #52 (CC), 3 (4, 4, 4, 5) skeins; Garnet Red Heather #1409, Ash #54, and Rust Heather #9427, 1 skein each

- Size 7 (4.5mm), 32"/81.5cm long circular needle and double-pointed needles or size needed to obtain gauge
- Size 6 (4mm) 32"/81.5cm long circular needle and double-pointed needles
- Six buttons
- Stitch markers
- Waste yarn or stitch holders
- Tapestry needle

Gauge
18.25 sts and 21 rows = 4"/10cm in St st on larger needle
Adjust needle size as necessary to obtain the correct gauge.

SPECIAL TECHNIQUES

Increase Methods

Neat and easy inc: K2, kfb, knit to last 3 sts, kfb, k2.

Symmetrical left and right leaning inc: K2, M1L, knit to last 2 sts, M1R, k2.

STITCH PATTERNS

Seed stitch:

Row 1: *K1, p1; rep from * to end.

Row 2: *P1, k1; rep from * to end.

Rep Rows 1 and 2 for seed st.

Stockinette stitch (worked in-the-round):

Knit every row.

24

INSTRUCTIONS

With Blacksheep, using smaller 32"/81cm long circular needle with long-tail or German twisted method, CO 161 (173, 187, 205, 223) sts. Pm at beg of rnd and join, taking care not to twist sts.

Lower Hem

Rnd 1: K7 (steek sts), pm, work in seed st to first marker.

Rep Rnd 1, moving markers as you come to them, until hem measures 2"/5cm—154 (166, 180, 198, 216) sts, not counting 7 steek sts.

Body

With larger 32"/81cm long circular needle, work in St st (knit every rnd) for 3 rnds.

Foll Hem Chart for 11 rnds.

Note: This should measure 3"/7.5cm; if not, add a few rows St st in MC so piece measures 5"/12.5cm from beg.

With MC, work in St st until total body length is 15 (16, 17, 18, 19)"/38 (40.5, 43, 45.5, 48.5)cm.

Leave the body sts on needle and work sleeves.

Sleeves

With Blacksheep and smaller dpns, CO 31 (35, 35, 39, 39) sts. Pm at beg of rnd and join, taking care not to twist sts. Work in seed st for 1.5"/4cm, working M1 at the end of the last rnd—32 (36, 36, 40, 40) sts.

Note: The foll instructions are worked AT THE SAME TIME and you are switching needles, so please read through before beg.

With larger dpns, work chart for cuff in St st; at the same time, work incs in either method below. After Rnd 6 you will have 2 extra sts in MC near the marker. These are intentional, just work them in MC and work the color chart around them for the next 3 rnds.

Using either "neat and easy inc" or "symmetrical left and right leaning inc" method, inc 1 st each side every 6 (6, 6, 6, 5) rnds 12 (12, 14, 15, 18) times—56 (60, 64, 70, 76) sts.

Note: Sleeve length to underarm should be 17 (17, 17.5, 17.5, 18)"/43 (43, 44.5, 44.5, 45.5)cm. If you have not reached that length, work a few more rnds.

Place 12 (14, 14, 16, 16) sts on a holder or waste yarn for underarm (these should be centered on your marker so that 6 [7, 7, 8, 8] sts are to the left of the marker and 6 [7, 7, 8, 8] sts are to the right of the marker)—44 (46, 50, 54, 60) sts rem. Leave a 20"/51cm tail for sewing later.

Work 2nd sleeve in the same manner.

Yoke

Note: Connect the sts of the body and the sleeves together with the 32"/81.5cm long needle and the yarn attached to the body piece to start the base of the yoke, setting aside dpns when you come to them.

On the body, using larger 32"/81.5cm long needle and starting at beg marker, k7 (steek), sm, k32 (34, 38, 41, 44) sts for right front; place next 12 (14, 14, 16, 16) sts on a holder or waste yarn for underarm; with underarm sts of right body and sleeve on hold facing each other k44 (46, 50, 54, 60) right sleeve sts; at back right of body work first body st after underarm and k66 (70, 76, 84, 96) sts for back, put next 12 (14, 14, 16, 16) sts of body on a holder or waste yarn for underarm; with underarm sts of left body and sleeve on hold facing each other k44 (46, 50, 54, 60) left sleeve sts; then k32 (34, 38, 41, 44) sts for left front—218 (230, 252, 274, 304) sts.

On next rnd, knit and dec 2 (2, 0, 4, 4) sts evenly across—216 (228, 252, 270, 300) sts.

With MC, work St st in-the-round for 0 (1, 1, 1.5, 1.5)"/0 (3, 3, 4, 4)cm.

Work Upper Icelandic Chart, working decs when they are indicated.

When chart is complete, there should be 72 (76, 84, 90, 100) sts.

On next rnd, with Blacksheep, work the foll dec, changing to to dpns with necessary:

For size Small: (K7, k2tog) 8 times—64 sts.

For size Medium: (K7, k2tog) 8 times, end k4—68 sts.

For size Large: (K5, k2tog) 12 times—72 sts.

For size XLarge: (K4, k2tog) 15 times—75 sts.

For size XXLarge: (K3, k2tog) 20 times—80 sts.

Change to smaller dpns and, with Blacksheep, work in seed st for 1"/2.5cm. BO loosely in pat.

Sewing and Cutting the Steek

It helps to baste a line of contrasting-colored yarn along the sts you will be sewing as a guide. With a sewing machine, sew four lines (refer to steek chart):

up st #1 and down st #2, up st #7 and down st #6. Then carefully cut through st #4.

Button Band

With smaller circular needle and Blacksheep, pick up 3 sts for every 4 rows, making sure to end with an odd number. Work back and forth in seed st as foll:

Row 1: K1, *p1, k1; rep from * to end.

Row 2: K1, *p1, k1; rep from * to end.

Rep Rows 1 and 2 for 1"/2.5cm. BO.

Place markers for six buttons evenly spaced on button band with first one 1"/2.5cm from CO edge and the 6th one to be worked in the neckband.

Buttonhole Band

Work same as for Button Band, placing buttonholes opposite markers when band measures ½"/1.25cm as foll:

PATTERN NOTES

- The steek for this pattern consists of 7 stockinette sts worked in MC only for uncharted parts of the pattern. For the charted part, see Icelandic Steek Chart, which will be worked in the beginning of the rnd before other charts are worked.

- Switching colors for the next rnd in the middle of this steek is helpful because you will not need to sew in ends and can avoid a jog in your join. For example, use the last rnd(s) color with MC for sts #1, #2, and #3—switch colors and knit with the new color and MC for sts #4, #5, #6, and #7.

- The colors used for striping in the steek are not particularly vital, so if you get a few switched, don't worry.

- When sewing the steek, you will be machine sewing four lines with a sewing machine: up st #1, and down st #2, up st #7, and down st #6. Then carefully cut through st #4.

- To make a pullover style, omit the 7 steek sts and skip the Icelandic Steek Chart throughout.

- Try to hold your colors loosely while working the color patterns to avoid puckering.

- Some people have a looser gauge in seed st; if you do not, use the same size 7 needle throughout project.

- The sleeves can be knit using magic loop method or double-pointed needles.

- Sections of charts circled in red are repeated.

- Adding short rows to give length to the back of the sweater is highly suggested and will improve your fit greatly!

- Short rows can be added at the base of the hem just before joining sleeves and body, and/or just after the yoke pattern at the neck.

- Please note that the sleeve increase and color chart for the cuff are worked at the same time. Therefore, please read through the instructions before beginning.

Buttonhole row: *Work to marker, after a purl st (k2tog yo); rep from * across all markers, work to end of row.

Cont in seed st until band measures 1"/2.5cm. BO.

Sew on buttons.

FINISHING

Graft tog the sts held at the underarms using Kitchener st.

Tack the edge of steek down by hand sewing. Weave in ends. Block.

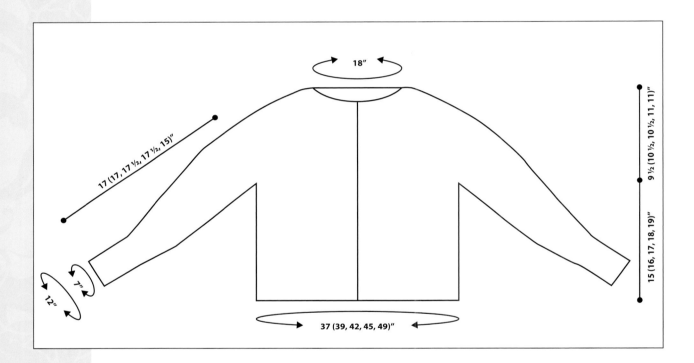

18"

17 (17, 17 ½, 17 ½, 15)"

9 ½ (10 ½, 10 ½, 11, 11)"

15 (16, 17, 18, 19)"

7"

12"

37 (39, 42, 45, 49)"

Cuff Chart

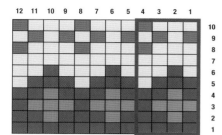

Columns: 12 11 10 9 8 7 6 5 4 3 2 1
Rows: 10 9 8 7 6 5 4 3 2 1

Hem Chart

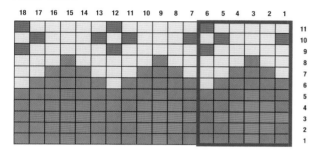

Columns: 18 17 16 15 14 13 12 11 10 9 8 7 6 5 4 3 2 1
Rows: 11 10 9 8 7 6 5 4 3 2 1

KEY

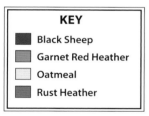

- ■ Black Sheep
- ■ Garnet Red Heather
- □ Oatmeal
- ■ Rust Heather

Upper Yoke Chart

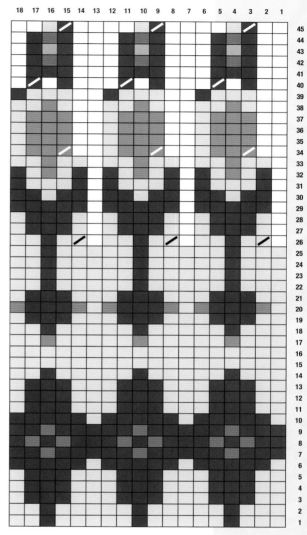

Columns: 18 17 16 15 14 13 12 11 10 9 8 7 6 5 4 3 2 1
Rows: 45 44 43 42 41 40 39 38 37 36 35 34 33 32 31 30 29 28 27 26 25 24 23 22 21 20 19 18 17 16 15 14 13 12 11 10 9 8 7 6 5 4 3 2 1

KEY

- ■ Black Sheep
- ■ Garnet Red Heather
- □ Oatmeal
- ■ Rust Heather
- □ No Stitch
- ◢ K2tog: Using color indicated, knit two stitches together as one stitch
- ■ Ash

Steek Chart

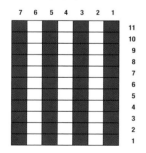

Columns: 7 6 5 4 3 2 1
Rows: 11 10 9 8 7 6 5 4 3 2 1

KEY

- ■ MC
- □ CC

ICELANDIC FIMMVÖRÐUHÁLS SWEATER

DESIGN BY HÉLÈNE MAGNÚSSON

The sweater is named after Fimmvörðuháls, a mountain pass in Iceland at the site of the now-famous eruption of the Eyjafjallajökull in 2010. I knitted this sweater during one of my Hiking and Knitting Tours that goes through the pass, between the two glaciers, and over the two new craters and the recently formed lava. I knitted while walking, holding the skein under my armpit, just like in the old days when Icelandic men and women knitted while walking from one farm to another or when working around in the fields. This sweater is typical of an Icelandic lopi yoke sweater. Although the tradition, which dates from the 1970s, is quite new, the sweater also draws inspiration from older Icelandic knitting traditions. The close-fitted shaping and the unusual elbow shaping can be found in old Icelandic knitted jackets. The colorwork in the yoke is faked with an undulating lace pattern, typical of Icelandic shawls. The crocheted chain bind-off, also very common in the old shawls, adds a feminine touch. Finally, the colors are reminicent of the Eyjafjallajökull glacier and the dirty ice that covers the ashes. ❧

Sizes
Adult XSmall (Small, Medium, **Large**, XLarge, XXLarge, XXXLarge)

Finished Measurements (slim fit)
Bust: 27.5 (30, 34.5, **36.5**){41, 46, 49.5}"/69 (75.5, 86.5, 91){102, 115.5, 124.5}cm
Waist: 20.5 (23, 27.5, 29.5){33.5, 39, 42.5}"/ 51 (57.5, 69, 73.5){84.5, 98, 106.5}cm
Length: 21.5 (22.5, 23.25, 24){25.5, 27, 28}"/54.5 (57, 59, 61){65, 68.5, 71}cm
Sleeve length to underarm: 17 (17.5, 18, 18){18.5, 18.5, 18.5}"/ 43 (44, 45, 46){47, 47, 47}cm

Materials ❨4❩
◆ ístex *Létt-Lopi* (also Reynolds *Létt-Lopi*), 100% pure Icelandic wool, 50g/1.75oz, 109yds/100m per skein: Natural White #0051 (MC), 6 (7, 7, 8){8, 9, 9} skeins; Ash Heather Grey #0054 (CC1), Grey Heather #0057 (CC2), 1 skein each

◆ Size 7 (4.5mm) 24"/60cm long circular needle or size needed to obtain gauge
◆ Size 5 (3.75mm) 24"/60cm long circular needle
◆ Magic loop is used for smaller diameters (you can also use double-pointed needles)
◆ Size G-6/(4mm) crochet hook
◆ Stitch markers
◆ Waste yarn or stitch holders
◆ Tapestry needle

Gauge
18 sts and 24 rows = 4"/10cm in St st using larger needle
Adjust needle size as necessary to obtain correct gauge.

SPECIAL TECHNIQUES

Crocheted chain bind-off: Using crochet hook, sl st required number of sts together (insert hook through loops of sts as if to knit them together through the back loops, yarn over hook, and pull through all sts), *ch required number of sts, sl st required number of sts together*; rep from * to * across.

PATTERN NOTES

♦ The body and the sleeves are knit in-the-round in stockinette stitch. The body is shaped with a darted waist. At the armhole, the sts of the body and the sleeves are combined on one needle and the yoke is knit in-the-round. The shoulders and back are knitted longer by using short rows to lower the neckline.

♦ For proper shaping and to compensate for blocking in lace pattern st, the larger needle is used for the stockinette stitch work and the smaller needle for the lace yoke.

♦ Short rows are made using the yarn over (yo) method. On the RS, a yo is made by bringing the yarn to the front. On the WS, a yo is made by bringing the yarn to the back. When closing the gaps, the yo and the st on the other side of the gap are knitted together in such manner that the yo is under the st: as ssk if the yo is on the left on the gap, and as k2tog if the yo is on the right of the gap. If you feel more comfortable with the wrap and turn method, simply read the instructions "turn, yo" as "w&t" and pick up the wraps the way you are used to.

♦ Grafting or Kitchener stitch is used to join together two sets of live sts with a tapestry needle to create a row that looks like knit sts between them. The underarms are joined this way. Alternatively, you can bind off on the wrong side on three needles, or even bind off and sew.

♦ A provisional cast-on and a crocheted chain bind-off are used to make the loops at the bottom of the body and the hems.

INSTRUCTIONS

Sleeves

With MC and larger needle, CO 32 (36, 40, 46){50, 54, 60}sts using a provisional cast-on. Join, taking care not to twist sts, pm at end of rnd.

Next rnd: Knit 1 rnd in St st.

Eyelet rnd: (K2tog, yo) until end of rnd.

Cont in St st and start sleeve shaping, working incs and elbow shaping AT THE SAME TIME as foll:

Rnds 1–13 (13, 14, 14){14, 11, 11}: Work in St st.

Rnd 14 (14, 15, 15){15, 12, 12}: K1, M1, knit to 1 st before end of rnd, M1, knit rem st.

Rep these 14 (14, 15, 15){15, 12, 12} rnds 6 (6, 6, 6){6, 8, 8} times in all—44 (48, 52, 58){62, 70, 76} sts; AT THE SAME TIME, in the rnd following the 3rd inc rnd (or when sleeve length reaches the elbow), work elbow shaping with short rows: k28 (31, 34, 39){42, 45, 50}, turn, yo, p18 (20, 22, 26){28, 30, 34}, turn, yo, (k to 3 sts before gap, turn, yo, p to 3 sts before gap, turn, yo) twice.

In next rnd, close all the gaps (see Pattern Notes): Knit the first 3 yos with next st as k2tog, and next 3 yos with st before as ssk.

When sleeve measures 17 (17.5, 18, 18){18.5, 18.5, 18.5}"/43 (44, 45, 46){47, 47, 47}cm or when reaching desired length, k40 (44, 47, 53){56, 64, 69} and place next 8 (8, 10, 10){12, 12, 14} underarm sts on a st holder or length of yarn—36 (40, 42, 48){50, 58, 62} sts.

Break off a long length of yarn for use later to graft the underarms. Set sleeve aside and work 2nd sleeve in the same manner.

Body

With MC and larger needle, CO 124 (136, 156, 164){184, 208, 224} sts using a provisional cast-on. Pm at beg of rnd and join, taking care not to twist sts.

Next rnd: Knit in St st.

Eyelet rnd: (K2tog, yo) to end of rnd.

Cont in St st for 10 (12, 14, 16){18, 20, 22} rnds or desired length, placing 4 markers on last rnd as foll: k15 (17, 19, 20){23, 26, 28}, pm, k32 (34, 40, 42){46, 52, 56}, pm, k35 (39, 45, 47){53, 60, 65}, pm, k22 (24, 26, 28){32, 36, 38}, pm, knit rem 20 (22, 26, 27){30, 34, 37} sts.

Waist Shaping

Decs

Rnd 1–7: Work in St st.

Rnd 8: (Knit to 3 sts before next marker, ssk, k2, k2tog) 4 times, knit to end of rnd.

Rep these 8 rnds 4 times in all—92 (104, 124, 132){152, 176, 192} sts.

Work 4 (4, 4, 4){5, 5, 5} rnds even.

Incs

Rnd 1: (Knit to 1 st before next marker, M1, k2, M1) 4 times, knit to end of rnd—124 (136, 156, 164){184, 208, 224} sts.

Rnds 2–10: Work in St st.

Rep these 10 rnds 4 times in all—124 (136, 156, 164) {184, 208, 224}sts.

Cont until body measures 14.5 (15, 15.5, 16){17, 18, 18.5}"/37 (38, 39, 41){43, 45, 47}cm or when reaching desired length. Remove back markers but **not** front markers.

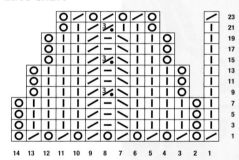

Yoke

Combine the body and the sleeves on the larger needle as foll:

Knit sts of body to 4 (4, 5, 5){6, 6, 7} sts before end of rnd, set next 8 (8, 10, 10){12, 12, 14} sts on a st holder (underarm sts); with yarn from the body, k36 (40, 42, 48){50, 58, 62} sts of left sleeve, k54 (60, 68, 72){80, 92, 98} sts of body front, set next 8 (8, 10, 10){12, 12, 14} sts on a st holder (underarm sts), k36 (40, 42, 48){50, 58, 62} sts of left sleeve, k54 (60, 68, 72){80, 92, 98} rem sts of body back, pm at end of rnd—180 (200, 220, 240){260, 300, 320} sts.

Knit 1 rnd.

Work the shoulders and back longer in order to lower the neckline, using short rows, as follows:

Knit to left front marker, turn, yo, purl back to right front marker, turn, yo, *knit to 3 sts before gap, turn, yo, purl to 3 sts before gap, turn, yo*; rep from * to * 4 (4, 4, 5){5, 5, 5} times.

Next rnd: Close gaps (see Pattern Notes): knit the 5 (5, 5, 6){6, 6, 6} left front yos with the next st as k2tog, and the 5 (5, 5, 6){6, 6, 6} right front yos with the st before as ssk.

Knit 1 (1, 2, 3){3, 4, 4} rnds.

Dec rnd: [(K1, k2tog) 6 times, k2] 9 (10, 11, 12){13, 15, 16} times—126 (140, 154, 168){182, 210, 224} sts.

Knit 1 rnd, change to smaller needle.

Foll Lace St Chart (note that only uneven rnds are marked; all even rnds are knit).

Work Rnds 1–2 with MC, Rnds 3–9 with CC1, Rnds 10–15 with CC2, Rnds 16–21 with CC1, Rnds 22–24 with MC.

Knit 2 rnds.

BO using a crocheted chain bind-off (see Pattern Notes): *Sl 3 sts, ch 4; rep from * until all sts are worked. Close rnd with a sl st, break off yarn.

Note: Some sizes will end, sl 2 sts once or twice.

Finishing

Graft underarm sts. Remove provisional cast-on at the bottom of the body and the sleeves and set sts on needle. BO with a crocheted chain bind-off (see Pattern Notes) using MC: *sl 3 sts, ch 4; rep from * until all sts are worked.

Note: Some sizes will end sl 2 sts once or twice. When all sts are worked, close rnd with a sl st, break off yarn.

Hand wash the sweater delicately in lukewarm water with gentle wool soap. Pin the lace yoke and leave the sweater to dry flat.

Lace Chart

(rows numbered 23, 21, 19, 17, 15, 13, 11, 9, 7, 5, 3, 1; columns 14 13 12 11 10 9 8 7 6 5 4 3 2 1)

KEY

Knit
(RS) Knit
(WS) Purl

k2tog
(RS) Knit 2 stitches together
(WS) Purl 2 together

Purl
(RS) Purl
(WS) Knit

p3tog
(RS) Purl 3 together
(WS) Knit 3 stitches together

ssk
(RS) slip, slip, knit slipped sts together
(WS) slip, slip, purl slipped sts together

No stitch
(RS) No stitch
(WS) No stitch

Yarn over
(RS) Yarn over
(WS) Yarn over

SWEDISH ULLARED PULLOVER

DESIGN BY BETH BROWN-REINSEL

This garment is a modern reproduction of the sweater in the Nordiska Museet in Stockholm, Sweden, dated 1898. It has been designed with more ease and a wider neck than the original. The body is worked in-the-round from the bottom ribbing to the neckline without additional stitches for steeks. The shoulder area is worked back and forth flat. The armholes are sewn and cut, contrary to the original sweater, but more to modern knitting tastes. The sleeves are worked from the shoulder to the cuff in-the-round, separately, with facings to hide the raw seams, again adjusting for the modern knitter. The sleeves were traditionally knitted separately and sewn in later without a facing, as no raw edge from cutting was present. This made knitting while on the go much easier, as opposed to lugging an entire sweater along while finishing up the sleeves. ❧

Sizes
Adult Small (Medium, **Large**, XLarge, XXLarge)

Finished Measurements
Chest: **38** (44, 50, 56.5)"/96.5 (112, 127, 144)cm
Length: 24.5"/62cm

Materials 1
◆ Rauma *Finullgarn* (100% wool, 50g/1.75oz, 180yds/165m per skein: Red #418, 6 (6, 7, 8) skeins; Black #436, 6 (7, 7, 8) skeins

◆ Size 0 (2mm) 32"/81.5cm long circular needle
◆ Size 1 (2.25mm) 16"/40.5cm and 32"/81.5cm long circular and double-pointed needles or size needed to obtain gauge
◆ Size 5 (1.75mm) steel crochet hook
◆ Stitch markers
◆ Waste yarn or stitch holders

Gauge
31 sts and 36 rnds = 4"/10cm in 2-color St st on larger needles. *Adjust needle size as necessary to obtain correct gauge.*

PATTERN NOTE

This sweater is knitted in-the-round from the ribbing to the neckline. Adjustments to length in the body and sleeves can be easily made within the main body and sleeve motif areas, although on the body this may affect the balance of the bordering negative motifs. One full repeat of the patterning (8 rnds) equals 1"/2.5cm. For men's sizing, the sleeves should measure approximately 18 (19, 19, 20)"/45.5 (48.5, 48.5, 51)cm from cuff edge to beg of the facing. There are seam sts that should be maintained up the entire length of the garment: 2 black, 2 red, 2 black. The beginning of the rnd begins in the middle of one seam (see Main Body Motif Chart).

INSTRUCTIONS

Body

Ribbing

With black and red yarn and smaller circular needle, CO 288 (336, 384, 432) sts with the long-tail cast-on method, holding the red yarn over your thumb and the black yarn over your left forefinger. (The sts will be black, with a red ridge.) Pm at beg of rnd and join, taking care not to twist sts.

You can loosely strand the unused color up the inside of the garment while working the striped ribbing, instead of cutting the yarns to avoid excess ends.

Work in (k3, p1) ribbing as foll (see Striped Ribbing Chart):

Rnds 1–9: Black.

Rnds 10–12: Red.

Rnds 13–14: Black.

Rnds 15–19: Red.

Rnds 20–21: Black.

Rnds 22–24: Red.

Rnds 25–28: Black.

Change to 32"/81.5cm long larger circular needle and knit 1 black rnd, inc 6 sts evenly—294 (342, 390, 438) sts.

Lower Body

Border Motif Chart

Rnd 1: *Work Border Motif Chart across 147 (171, 195, 219) sts, working the 6-st rep 23 (27, 31, 35) times with 5 sts before first rep and 4 sts after last rep as shown on chart; pm for the midpoint of rnd; rep from * once.

Rnds 2–9: Work all 9 rnds of the chart.

Main Body Motif Chart

Rnd 1: *Work Main Body Motif Chart across 147 (171, 195, 219) sts, working the 6-st rep 20 (24, 28, 32) times with 11 sts before first rep and 16 sts after last rep as shown on chart for Front; rep from * for Back.

Rnds 2 and 3: Foll chart, work Rnds 2 and 3.

Work chart Rnds 4–27 three times.

Work chart Rnds 4–7 once.

On next rnd, the initial/date box will be started. Insert Initial/Date Box, Alphabet, or Flower as foll:

Initial/Date Box, Alphabet, or Flower Motif Chart

The initial/date box can be filled in with the initials of the intended wearer of the sweater as well as the year, as the original Ullareds were designed. Alternatively, you can use the Flower Motif Chart.

Work across 58 (70, 82, 94) sts in est pat; beg with Rnd 1 of Initial/Date Box Chart (31 sts wide) on the Front only, keeping rest of the patterning as est. When you have worked the 25 rnds of the Box chart, resume the Main Body Motif Chart as est.

Note: You should be ready to work Rnd 9 of the Main Body Motif Chart.

Work up through Rnd 27, then work Rnds 28–31 once.

Neck and Shoulder Motif

Rnds 1–8: Work Rnds 1–8 of Border Motif Chart.

Rnd 9: Using only black yarn, BO 2 red seam sts, work across 49 (57, 65, 77) sts, BO 47 (55, 63, 63) sts, work across 49 (57, 65, 77) sts, BO 2 red seam sts; work across Back sts in black dec 0 (dec 4, inc 2, dec 2) sts evenly [145 (165, 195, 215) Back sts]. Turn work.

Back Shoulders

Note: Continue working back and forth across Back, beg with Row 1 of the Shoulder Motif Chart, for 17 rows as foll:

Row 1 (WS): Join red yarn, work 10-st rep 3 (4, 5, 6) times with 9 sts before first rep and 8 sts after last rep as shown on chart.

On Row 14, work across 49 (57, 65, 77) sts, BO 51 (51, 61, 61) sts, work across 47 (57, 67, 77) sts.

Rows 2–22: Cont working back and forth on one shoulder as est for rem rows foll Shoulder Motif Chart.

Put sts on waste yarn or holder.

Join yarn to other Back shoulder and finish Shoulder Motif Chart by working Rows 15–22.

Left Front Shoulder

With RS facing, join yarn to armhole edge of Left Shoulder and work across Shoulder Motif Chart for 47 (57, 67, 77) sts as foll:

Work first 8 sts of chart from right to left, then work rep until there are no more sts.

Note: You will not have worked the seam sts at the left side of the chart. Work back and forth as est through Row 22.

Put sts on waste yarn or holder.

Right Front Shoulder

Join yarn to the WS (armhole edge) and work across the 17 sts of the left side of the chart, then work the rep until there are no more sts.

Note: You will not have worked the seam sts at the right side of the chart. Work back and forth as est through Row 22.

Put sts on waste yarn or holder.

Sleeves (make 2)

Note: The sleeves are worked from the armhole to the cuff. There are sleeve seam sts (2 red, 2 black, 2 red) that foll the underside to the cuff.

With black yarn, CO 120 (138, 156, 174) sts onto a 16"/40.5cm long larger circular needle. Pm at beg of rnd and join, being careful not to twist sts. Work around in rev St st for 1"/2.5cm for sleeve facing.

Beg Rnd 1 of Sleeve Chart, joining red yarn and work even according to pat maintaining the 6-st seam (2 red, 2 black, 2 red) and 6-st rep 19 (22, 25, 28) times. When sleeve measures 2"/5cm from Rnd 1, beg shaping sleeve by dec 1 st at beg and end of rnds as foll:

Dec rnd: K1 black, k1 red, ssk in red, work across sleeve in pat to last 4 sts of rnd, k2tog in red, k1 red, k1 black.

Rep dec rnd every 5th rnd 13 (0, 0, 0) times, every 4th rnd 7 (17, 5, 0) times, every 3rd rnd 0 (12, 28, 27) times, every 2nd rnd 0 (0, 0, 15) times until 78 (78, 88, 88) sts rem and sleeve is approx 14.25 (15.25, 15.25, 16.25")/36 (39, 39, 41.5)cm long or 2.75" (7cm) less than desired length, dec 1 st at end of last rnd—77 (77, 87, 87) sts.

Work Cuff Motif A Chart.

Beg Cuff Motif B Chart (3-st rep), discontinuing the seam sts and dec 2 (2, 3, 3) sts evenly across first rnd—75 (75, 84, 84) sts. When the chart is completed, BO sts loosely.

Finishing

Wash and rinse the body and sleeves. Lay flat to dry. Weave in ends

Sewing and Cutting the Armholes

Measure the top of the sleeve just under the facing. Using that measurement, measure from the top of the shoulder down along the armhole edge to find the base of the armhole [approx 8 (9, 10.5, 11.5)"/20 (23, 26.5, 29)cm from top edge of body] and mark it with a piece of contrasting waste yarn. With a sewing machine, sew 1 line of stitching down the center of each of the 2 center red seam sts from the point where the 2 red sts were bound off, down to the base of the armhole. Sew horizontally below the point of each armhole. Then sew another line between the red sts and the adjacent black sts. You will have four lines of stitching at each armhole that look like a long "U." Be certain to backstitch at beg and end of each of these seams. Cut the knitting between the two red seam sts, being careful not to cut your machine stitching. Cut all the way to the horizontal stitching below each armhole, but do not cut through it.

Joining the Shoulders

Put sts from Right Front Shoulder on a dpn and sts from Right Back Shoulder onto another dpn. Holding the two needles tog as one in your left hand, with RS tog, work the 3-needle bind-off. Rep for Left Shoulder.

Sew sleeves to the body, matching the 6 seam sts at the base of the armhole with those on the underside of the sleeve—colors will oppose each other. Lightly block sleeve seams. Then, turning sweater inside out, loosely whip down edges of facing to inside of body, concealing cut edges of the armhole.

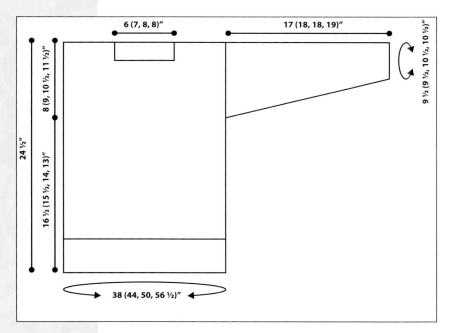

Twined Purled Edge

Note: Although this finish is not traditional to the Ullared, it is a lovely edge.

With smaller circular needle and black yarn, pick up 150 (166, 182, 182) sts around neck.

Rnd 1: Join the other end of the same black skein and purl the entire round, using one yarn, then bring the new yarn under the one just used to purl the next st. Break off one yarn.

Rnd 2: Knit and BO.

Alternative Crochet Edging

Using steel size 5 (1.75mm) crochet hook, work a crochet edge around the neck and the sleeve cuffs, in red, as foll:

Join yarn, *ch 1, sk 1, work 4 dc in one st, sk 1; rep from * around to beg of rnd. Break yarn.

Main Body Motif Chart

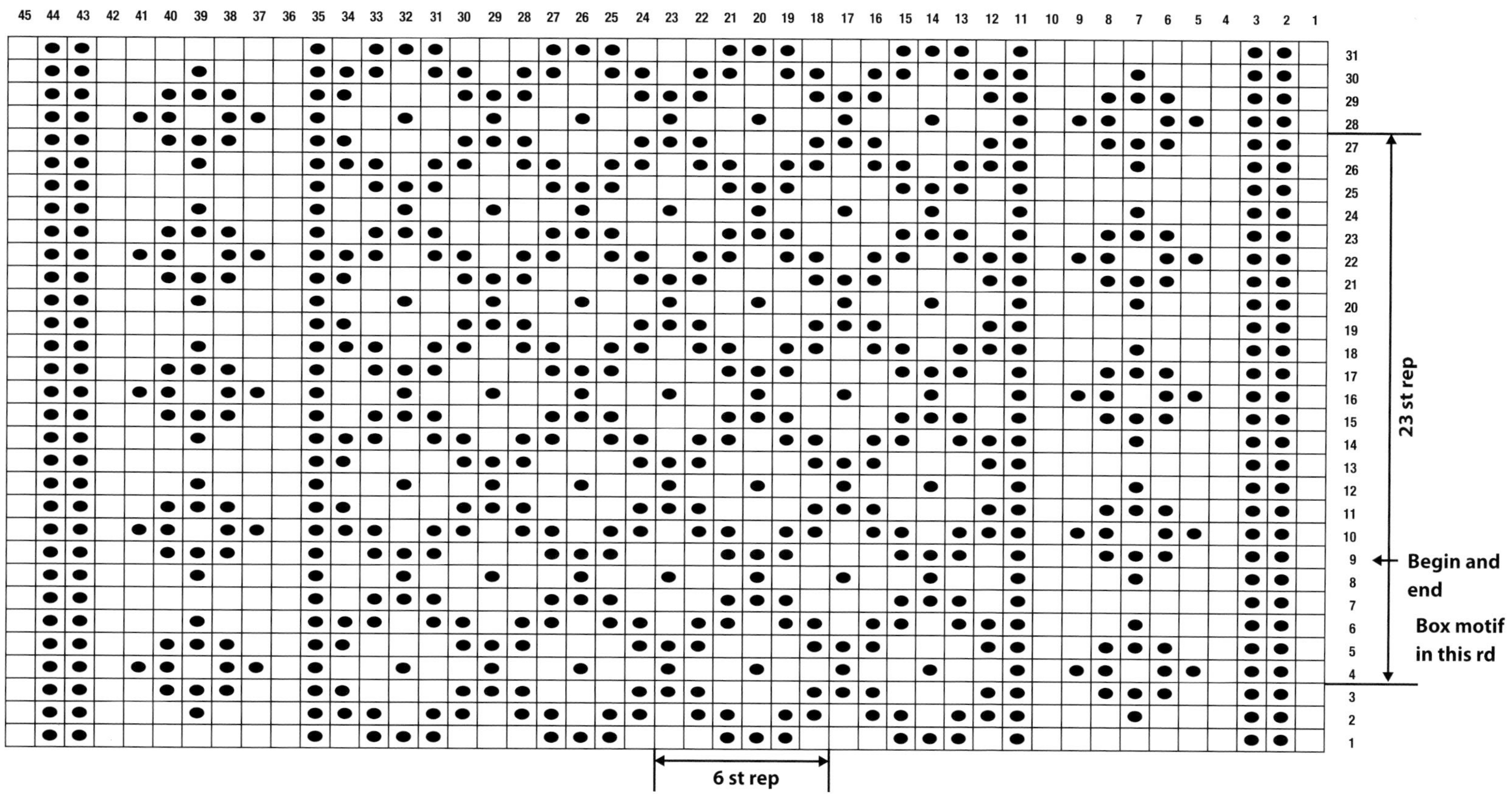

23 st rep

Begin and end

Box motif in this rd

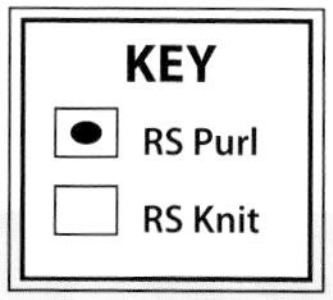

6 st rep

KEY
- ● RS Purl
- ☐ RS Knit

Striped Ribbing Chart

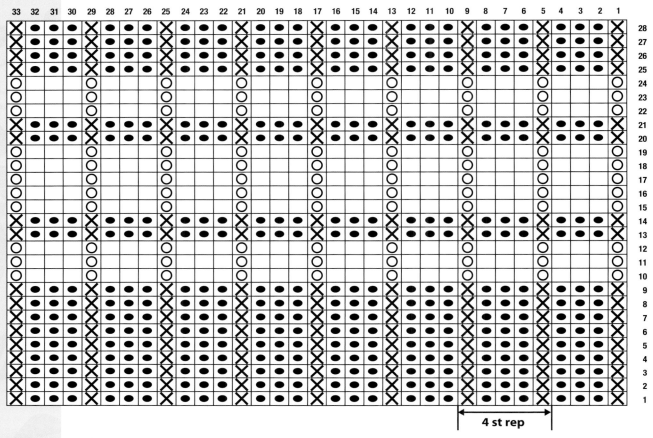

Shoulder Motif Chart

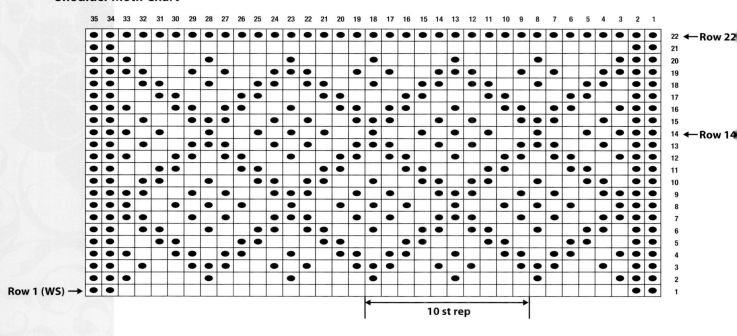

Initial/Date Box Chart

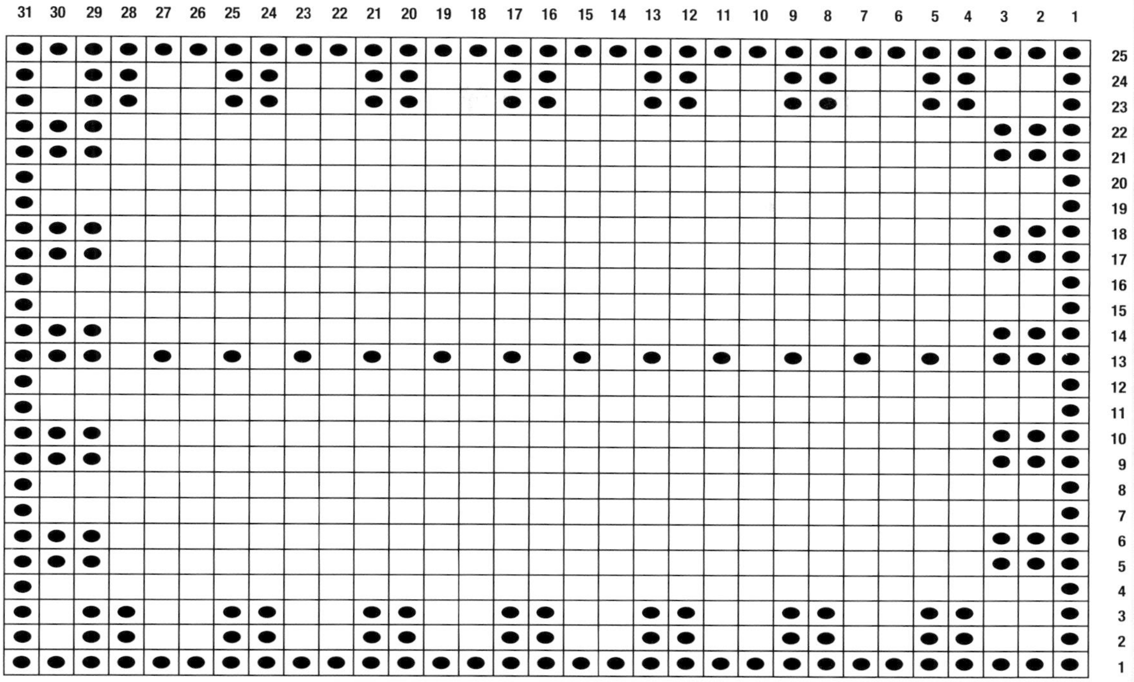

Flower Chart

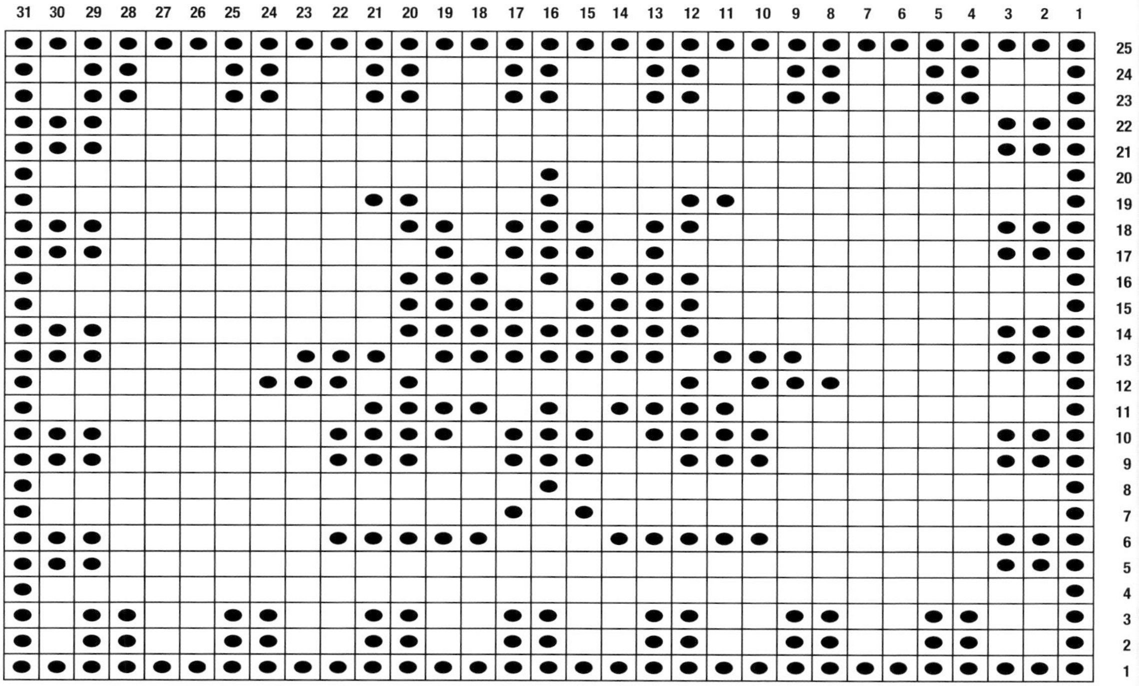

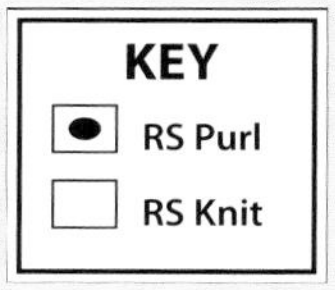

KEY
- ● RS Purl
- ☐ RS Knit

39

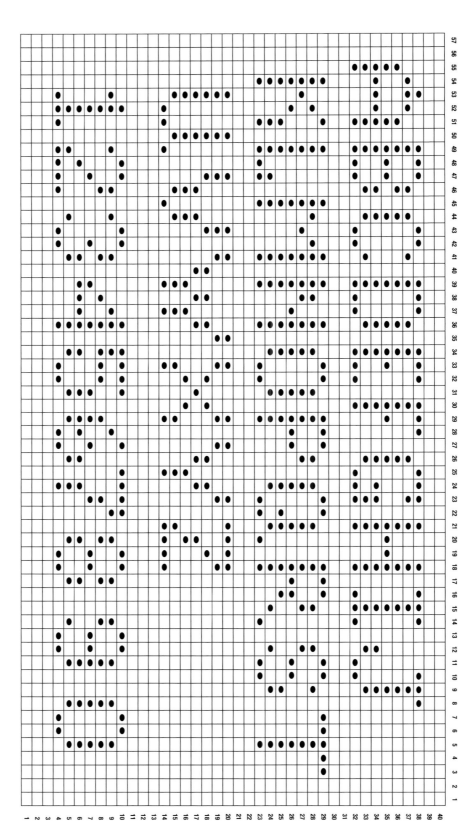

KEY
- ● RS Purl
- ☐ RS Knit

Sleeve Chart

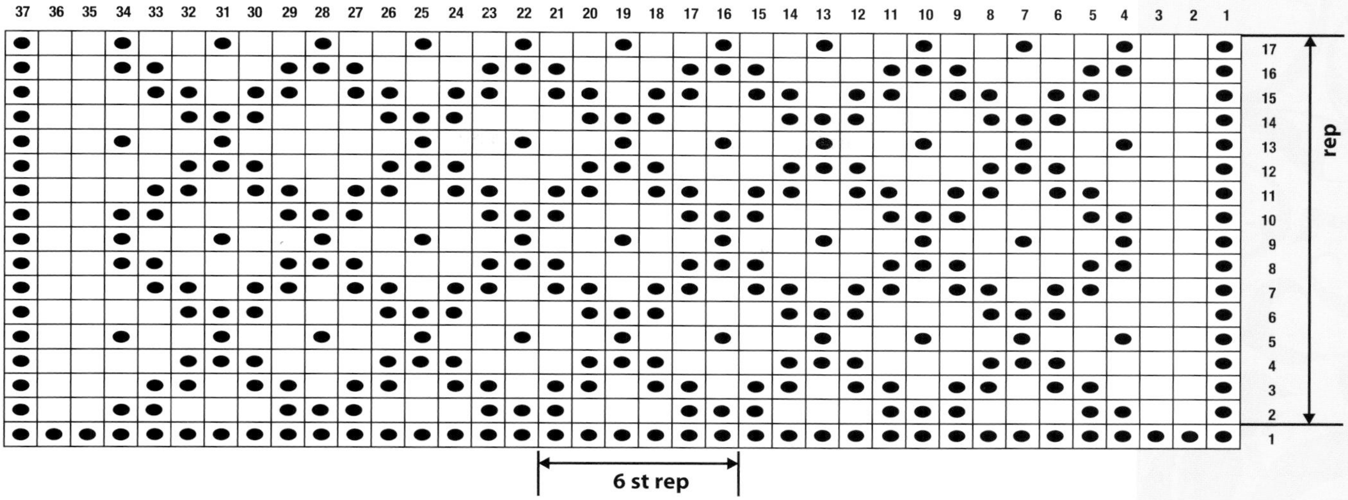

37 36 35 34 33 32 31 30 29 28 27 26 25 24 23 22 21 20 19 18 17 16 15 14 13 12 11 10 9 8 7 6 5 4 3 2 1

(rows numbered 1–17 on right, "rep" bracket)

6 st rep

Cuff Motif Chart A

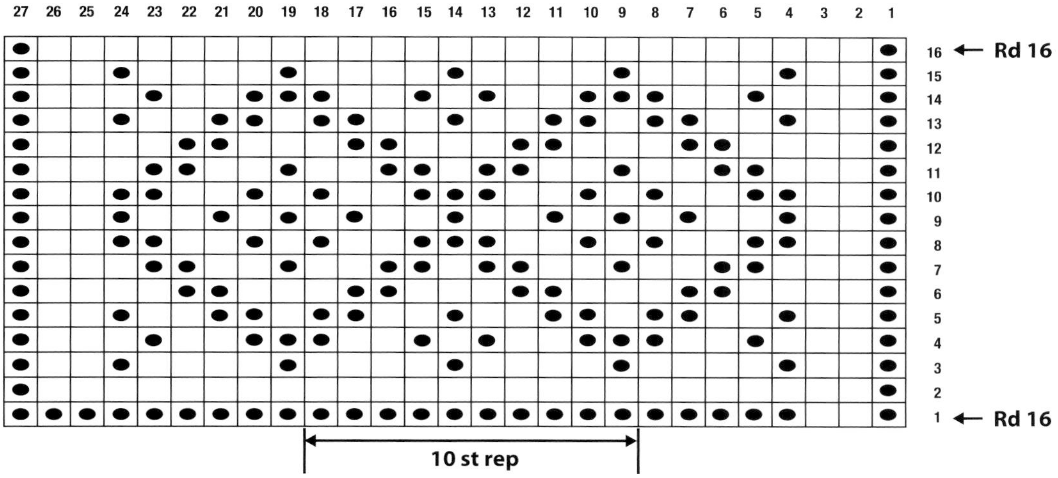

27 26 25 24 23 22 21 20 19 18 17 16 15 14 13 12 11 10 9 8 7 6 5 4 3 2 1

16 ← Rd 16

(rows numbered 1–16 on right)

1 ← Rd 16

10 st rep

Cuff Motif Chart B

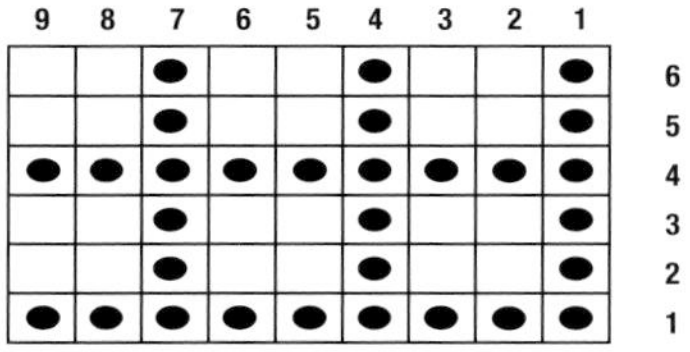

9 8 7 6 5 4 3 2 1

(rows numbered 1–6 on right)

Border Motif Chart

45 44 43 42 41 40 39 38 37 36 35 34 33 32 31 30 29 28 27 26 25 24 23 22 21 20 19 18 17 16 15 14 13 12 11 10 9 8 7 6 5 4 3 2 1

(rows numbered 1–9 on right)

6 st rep

41

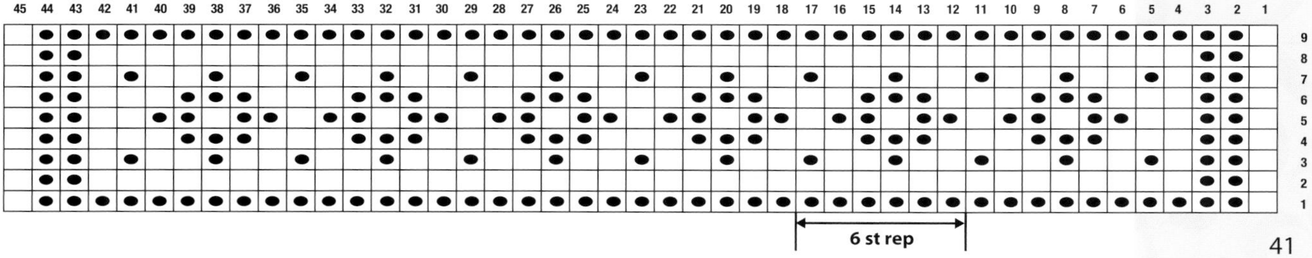

NORWEGIAN REIN AND SNOW SWEATER

DESIGN BY SUE FLANDERS

The classic Norwegian design elements of reindeer and snowflakes have been used in a patchwork pattern to make this cute child's sweater. The wide boatneck makes it easier to pull over the head and is a nice change from a ribbed neckline. ❧

Sizes
Child 4 (**8**, 12)

Finished Measurements
Chest: 25 (**29**, 32)"/63.5 (73.5, 81.5)cm
Length: 19 (20, 21)"/48.5 (51, 53.5)cm

Materials 〔 4 〕
◆ Cascade 220, 100% wool, 100g/3.5oz, 220yds/209m per skein: Blue #7817, 3 (3, 4) skeins; White #8305, 2 (2, 3) skeins

◆ Size 7 (4.5mm) double-pointed and 16"/40.5cm long circular needles
◆ Size 9 (5.5mm) double-pointed and 16"/40.5cm long circular needles or size needed to obtain gauge
◆ Stitch markers
◆ Waste yarn or stitch holders
◆ Tapestry needle

Gauge
19 sts and 16 rnds = 4"/10cm in stranded 2-color knitting with larger needle. *Adjust needle size as necessary to obtain correct gauge.*

PATTERN NOTES

The body is worked in-the-round, from the bottom up. Extra "steek" sts are added at the sides for armhole sewing. The steek stitches are sewn with a sewing machine and then cut to make the armhole opening.

INSTRUCTIONS

Body

With smaller circular needle and MC, CO 120 (136,152) sts. Pm for beg of rnd and join, taking care not to twist sts.

Work k1, p1 ribbing for 2.5 (3, 3.5)"/6.5 (7, 9)cm. Change to larger circular needle.

Knit 1 (3, 5) rnds; join CC.

Note: For Small size, there is no side chart, so just work Center Chart B. For the other sizes, use the appropriate chart for that size as indicated.

Set-up as foll: Work left side of Side Chart A as indicated, then Center Chart B once, then all of Chart A once and Center Chart B once, finishing with the right side of Chart A.

Cont to foll est charted pat until the indicated point for the "steek" sts. On this rnd, CO 5 sts at each underarm; these sts do not show on the chart, but will be worked as "ghost" sts for sewing later. Work the middle steek st in CC and the rest in MC. Work to the top of the chart and thread all sts onto the waste yarn.

Sleeves

With smaller dpns and MC, CO 34 (38, 44) sts. Pm for beg of rnd and join, taking care not to twist sts.

Work k1, p1 ribbing for 2.5"/6.5cm, M1, and pm in this st for center of sleeve.

Note: This st will always be worked in MC and is not shown on the chart.

Change to larger dpns, attach CC and foll Sleeve Chart, working M1 for incs on each side of marked st as shown on chart. Foll chart to top of sleeve as indicated for each size. Break off CC.

Knit 1 more rnd in MC.

Sleeve Facing

Cont sleeve sts working facing back and forth in reverse St st.

Rows 1 and 3: Purl.

Rows 2 and 4: Knit.

BO loosely, with larger needle.

Finishing

Set sewing machine to small sts. Place knitting under the machine foot and begin to sew on the CC set of sts. Sew to CO edge and turn, sew back along another row of sts. It is important not to sew the "ladders" between the sts, but to catch the sts where they are wrapped around each other. This will make a much stronger steek. Sew at least 3 rows on each side of the CC sts.

Shoulder Seams

Remove sts from the waste yarn and use 3-needle bind-off to join 15 (17, 19) sts on each side of the neck opening for shoulder seams leaving 30 (34, 38) sts for center neck each on the front and back of sweater.

Sleeve Attachment

In the sewn steek area, cut along the CC sts to open up the armhole. Sew sleeve into place along the line between steek sts and charted pat. Attach facing to the inside to cover the sewn edges.

Neckline

Place 30 (34, 38) sts on front waste yarn onto the larger dpns.

Attach MC and knit 1 row.

Row 1: CO 5 sts, purl.

Row 2: CO 5 sts, purl.

Row 3: Knit.

Row 4: Purl.

BO loosely.

Rep for back facing. Fold the facing to the inside of the sweater and tack it in. Use the 5 CO sts to reinforce the neckline corners.

Weave in all ends.

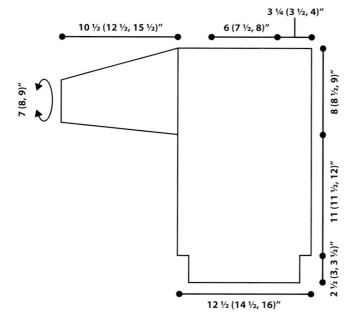

KEY

▨	Blue #7817 Knit RS
☐	White #8305 Knit RS
▮	Size 4
▯	Size 8

Side Charts

Side Chart A   **Center Chart B**

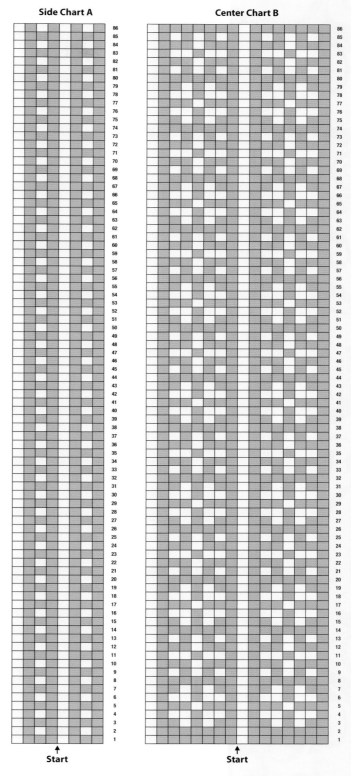

Start   Start

45

Main Body Chart

Sleeve Chart

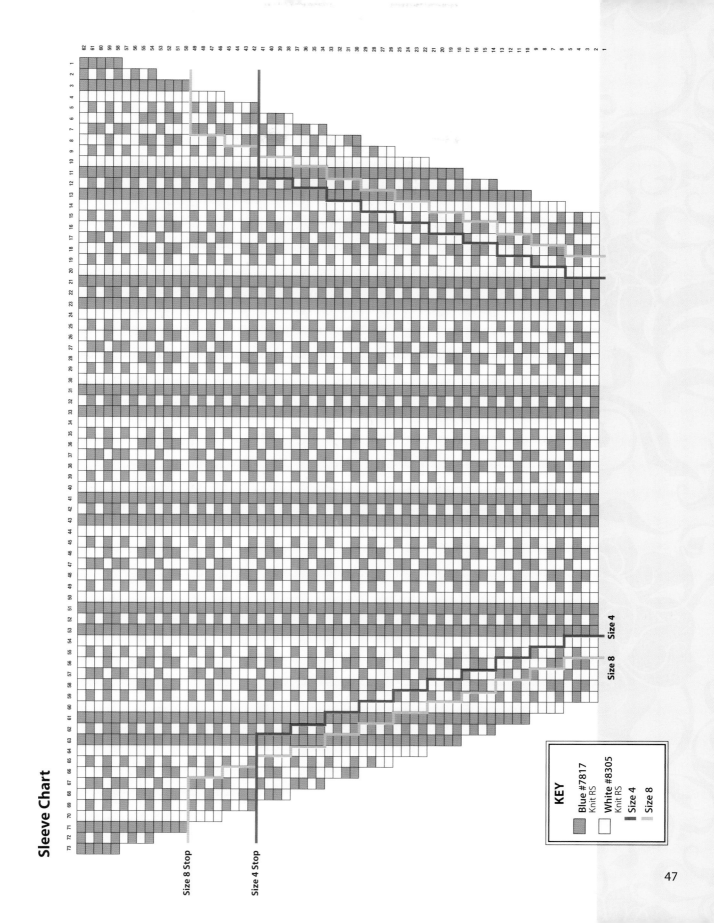

KEY

▨	Blue #7817 Knit RS
☐	White #8305 Knit RS
━	Size 4
━	Size 8

Size 8 Stop

Size 4 Stop

Size 4

Size 8

47

SWEATERS
OF EUROPE

Estonian Kihnu Troi Sweater

50

Bavarian Cropped Lattice Pullover

56

Bulgarian Roses Intarsia Cardigan

62

ESTONIAN KIHNU TROI SWEATER

DESIGN BY KATE LARSON

The Troi is a traditional sweater design from Kihnu, a tiny island off the coast of Estonia. Kihnu is a treasure trove of textile history and culture. Many people on the island still incorporate traditional dress into their everyday lives. The Troi is typically worn by men and can be spotted by eager textile travelers around the island and mainland Estonia. I have wonderful memories of seeing beautiful Troi sweaters in museum collections and on young men learning to play Kihnu folk music, and a modern Troi being knit on the short journey by ferry to the mainland port near Pärnu. Many older examples of Troi sweaters are white patterns on a background of hand-dyed indigo. Madder red bands are believed to provide the wearer with protection and well-being. ❧

Sizes
Adult Small (**Medium**, Large)

Finished Measurements
Chest: 38.5 (**44.75**, 51.25)"/98 (113.5, 130)cm
Length: 25.25 (27.5, 29)"/66.5 (70, 73.5)cm

Materials ❨ 1 ❩
◆ Elemental Affects *Shetland Fingering*, 100% North American Shetland Wool, 1oz/28g, 118yds/165m per skein: Baltic Blue #43 (MC1), 10 (11, 13) skeins; White (MC2), 9 (10, 12) skeins; Scarlet #39 (CC), 1 skein

◆ Size 2 (2.75mm), 32 (40, 40)"/81.5 (81.5, 101.5)cm and 16"/40.5cm long circular and double-pointed needles or size needed to obtain gauge
◆ Stitch markers
◆ Waste yarn or stitch holders
◆ Tapestry needle
◆ Scissors

Gauge
30 sts and 30 rows = 4"/10cm in Body Chart pat (blocked)
Adjust needle size as necessary to obtain correct gauge.

PATTERN NOTES

Read through entire pattern before beginning. Multiple sets of instructions happen simultaneously.

Charts are read as for knitting in-the-round; Work from right to left, bottom to top.

This sweater is primarily stockinette st knit in-the-round using two-color stranding techniques. Steek sts are added at the beginning of the armholes and neck edge. Shoulder bands are worked circularly on front sts only. Shoulder Steek sts are cut and live shoulder sts on circular needle are then attached to back sts using 3-needle bind-off to complete body.

The sleeves are knit from the armhole to cuff using sts picked up in pattern to form a seamless pattern shift from body to sleeve.

The Sleeve Chart shows only the right half of the sleeve. The other half of the sleeve is knit as a mirror image of this chart. The center st and seam st are outlined in red, indicating that these sts are not repeated. Rnd begins with seam st.

Finished measurements are based on the gauge of the sweater after blocking. Length measurements within instructions are finished measurements. Lightly stretch work to measure before blocking.

SPECIAL TECHNIQUES

Kihnu 2-color cast-on

Several two-color braided cast-on methods are used in Kihnu. The one used in this pattern can also be found in *Folk Knitting in Estonia* by Nancy Bush (Interweave Press, 2000). It is similar to a long-tail cast-on, but the front yarn is wrapped the opposite direction around the thumb (clockwise).

1. Begin by making two slipknots, one with dark color and one with light color, on the same needle. (Slipknots will be removed before joining in-the-round and will not be included in st count.)

2. Hold yarns as if to begin long-tail cast-on, with light yarn over thumb and dark yarn over index finger. Drop yarn off thumb and move thumb under light yarn, from front to back, so that the yarn is now wrapped the opposite direction. Thumb is between yarns.

INSTRUCTIONS

Body

With MC1, MC2, and longer circular needle, CO 288 (336, 384) sts using the Kihnu 2-color cast-on in color pat shown on Rnd 1 of Border Chart. Drop both slipknots and move first st of rnd to right needle. Pass 2nd st on right needle over first and drop off needle. Move rem st back to left needle, pm, and make sure the CO is not twisted before beg next row in the rnd.

Next rnd: *Beg with 3rd rnd of Border Chart, rep chart over 144 (168, 192) sts* for front and place underarm marker; rep from * to * for back.

Cont working Border Chart through Rnd 21. **Note:** When working vits, yarns will twist. Stop occasionally to untwist.

Next rnd: Beg Body Chart on Rnd 1 (13, 1). Rep chart to end of rnd, adding markers between pat reps if desired. Work a total of 103 (111, 119) rnds of Body Chart.

Piece measures about 15.75 (17, 18)"/40 (43, 45.5)cm from the CO edge, lightly stretched.

Armholes and Neck Shaping

Next rnd: Place first st of rnd on holder and CO 10 sts for steek with long-tail cast-on using MC1 and MC2 yarns, pm. Work in pat to next underarm marker, sm, place next st on holder, CO 10 sts for steek, pm, work in pat to end of rnd, sm, (k1 MC1, k1 MC2) twice, k1 MC1.

Note: End of rnd now falls in center of this steek. Place new end of rnd marker if desired.

Next rnd: Work 5 steek sts, (k1 MC1, k1 MC2) twice, k1 MC1, and sm, work in pat to next marker and rep steek color sequence for 2nd armhole steek, finish rnd in pat.

Cont in pat as est until 170 (182, 194) rnds have been worked and piece measures about 24.5 (26.5, 28)"/62 (67.5, 71)cm lightly stretched; AT THE SAME TIME, when 157 (169, 181) rnds have been worked, beg neck shaping as foll:

Work 5 steek sts, sm, work 51 (63, 73) sts in chart pat, pm, put next 41 (41, 45) sts on waste yarn or holder, CO 10 steek sts as before, pm and finish rnd in pat.

Next rnd (dec): Work in pat to 2 sts before neck steek, ssk, sm, work 10 steek sts, sm, k2tog, sm, and finish rnd in pat.

On next and 3 foll rnds, dec 1 st on each side of neck steek in this manner—46 (58, 68) body pat sts for each shoulder.

Work 1 rnd in pat without decs.

On next and 2 foll alternate rnds, dec 1 st each side of neck steek—43 (55, 65) body pat sts for each shoulder.

Work 1 more rnd in pat without shaping—170 (182, 194) rnds of Body Chart completed.

Shoulder Trim

Using MC1, MC2, CC, and shorter circular needle, beg working Rnd 3 of Border Chart as foll:

Work 5 steek sts, sm, work Border Chart beg with st indicated for size you are making to marker, sm, work 10 steek sts, work across right front as for left to marker, sm, and work first 5 sts of underarm steek—106 (130, 150) sts, including steeks that are now on shorter circular needle. Back sts remain on longer circular needle unworked. Join short needle for working in-the-rnd on front sts only and cont working Border Chart through Rnd 18.

Next rnd: Work Rnd 19 in chart as est, binding off all steek sts—43 (55, 65) sts on short circular needle. Break yarns.

Leaving sts on short circular needle, carefully cut open shoulder and neck steeks. (Do not cut armhole steeks yet.) Mark center 57 (57, 61) sts for back neck on longer body needle and turn garment inside out. With the front of the sweater facing you, attach dark yarn, and work rnd as follows: BO 5 steek sts from back, pass st on right needle back to left. Using 3-needle bind-off, BO 43 (55, 65) body and shoulder sts, BO 57 (57, 61) back neck sts, pass st on right needle back to left. Using 3-needle bind-off, BO 43 (55, 65) body and shoulder sts, BO 5 steeks sts from body. Turn garment RS out.

Left Sleeve

Cut armhole steeks. With short circular needle, MC1, and MC2, pick up and knit around each armhole opening as foll:

Beg with RS facing at underarm, knit underarm st on holder using MC1 (seam st), pick up sleeve sts from between the last body st and first steek st with yarn held behind the work, pickup sts are worked in pat, duplicating adjacent body sts at armhole edge (see first rnd of Sleeve Chart), cont to pick up 67 (71, 75) sts as described, pick up 9 sts in sleeve pat over shoulder trim, and cont pickup rnd as before down back armhole edge—144 (152, 160) sts. Place end of rnd marker.

Rnds 1–3: Beg working Sleeve Chart in-the-round, knitting first st of rnd in MC1 (seam st) throughout.

Dec rnd: K1 (seam st), k2tog, work in pat until 2 sts before marker, ssk.

Rep dec rnd every 4th rnd 33 (21, 27) times, then every 3rd rnd 2 (18, 10) times—74 (74, 86) sts.

Work 1 more rnd in pat without shaping.

Cuff

Beg on st indicated for size you are making, work Rnds 1–20 of Border Chart once, dec first and last st of Rnd 1—72 (72, 84) sts.

BO loosely with 2-color bind-off in pat shown on Border Chart Rnd 1.

Right Sleeve

Work as for Left Sleeve.

Finishing

Using MC1, CC, and shorter circular needle, beg picking up sts where left shoulder border meets back neck BO sts. Foll Border Chart Rnd 18, pick up and knit 17 sts along border, 15 sts down

3. Drop the needle tip down between yarns, lifting light yarn in back, near palm.

4. Pick up dark yarn as for long-tail cast-on. Needle tip then moves up through loop on thumb. Drop loop on thumb and tighten new st.

5. Switch yarns to begin next st by bringing dark yarn to front over light yarn. Work as before to cast on a light st.

Repeat until desired number of sts are cast on, plus 1 extra st for joining into the rnd, and 2 slipknot sts. Drop both slipknots and move first st of round to right needle. Pass 2nd st on right needle over first and drop off needle. Move remaining st back to left needle, place marker, and make sure the CO is not twisted before beginning the next row in-the-round.

Note: Yarns will twist when working this cast-on. Stop periodically to untwist.

Vits (two-color braid): Kihnu vits are worked in two colors, over two rnds. The first rnd is knit in alternating colors. Next rnd, bring yarns to front. Purl first st in opposite color as the previous rnd (e.g. knit a dark st with light yarn and a light st with dark yarn). Purl next st in opposite color, bringing yarnover yarn from previous st (counterclockwise). Continue to end of rnd.

Note: Yarns will twist. Stop periodically to untwist.

Steeks are sections of fabric that are cut open after knitting to create armholes, neck shaping, etc. They allow the knitter to continue working in-the-round throughout the piece. In this pattern, extra sts called steek sts are added where the fabric is later cut. This creates a facing that is folded back inside the work and sewn in place once the piece is finished.

3-needle bind-off: Bind off two pieces of knitting together, creating a seam. Hold both needles parallel, with RS together (WS facing). With 3rd needle of same size, insert needle knitwise into first st on front and back needles and k1. *K1 st into next st on front and back needles. Pass first st worked over 2nd and off needle. Rep from * across. Fasten off last st.

2-color bind-off: K1 st with opposite color (e.g. knit a dark st with light yarn and a light st with dark yarn), *k1 st with opposite color, pass first st over 2nd and off needle. Rep from * across. Fasten off last st.

Border Chart

KEY

- ☐ MC1
- ☐ MC2
- ■ CC
- ☐ Knit on right side
- ▬ Purl on right side
- ▼ Vits
- │ Begin hem, all sizes
  Begin S, M cuff
- │ Begin L cuff
- ▌ Begin S, M shoulder trim
- ▌ Begin L shoulder trim

front, 41 (41, 45) sts from holder, 15 sts up right front, 17 sts along border, and 57 (57, 61) back sts.

Note: End of rnd now falls at back left neck edge—162 (162, 170) neck sts.

Work Rnds 19 and 20 of Border Chart and BO loosely with 2-color bind-off in pat shown on Border Chart Rnd 1.

Weave in ends. Trim steeks and tack down.

Block to finished measurements on schematic.

Optional Fulling: If using Elemental Affects yarn, turn sweater inside out and put into washing machine on delicate in cold to warm water. This Shetland yarn felts very slowly, so a typical delicate cycle will just begin to full the fabric. As a result, the fabric will bloom and have a softer feel. Block to finished measurements on schematic.

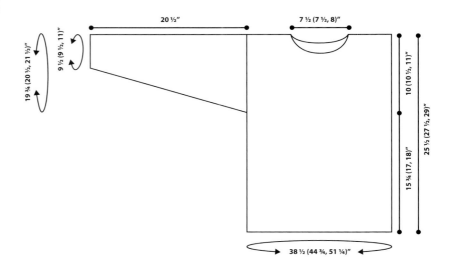

Body Chart

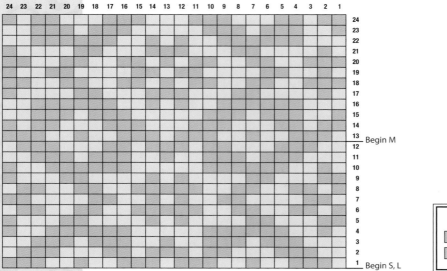

KEY

- ☐ MC1
- ☐ MC2

Sleeve Chart

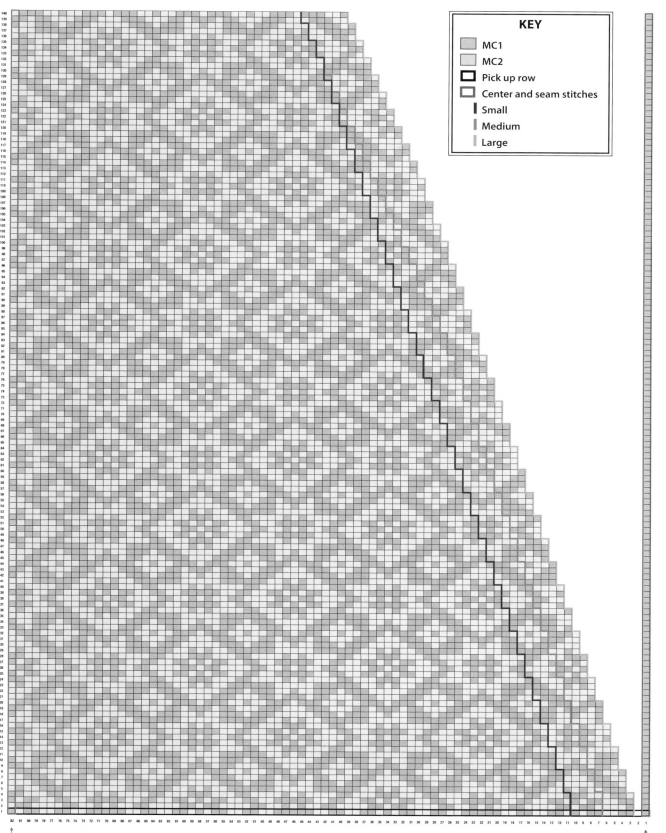

KEY

	MC1
	MC2
	Pick up row
	Center and seam stitches
	Small
	Medium
	Large

Center Stitch

Seam Stitch

BAVARIAN CROPPED LATTICE PULLOVER

DESIGN BY DONNA DRUCHUNAS

Bavarian twisted traveling stitches create a detailed texture that is similar to cable patterns but with finer lines and sharper stitch definition. This cropped pullover is inspired by the short, form-fitting jacket-sweaters worn by Bavarian and Austrian women with dirndl skirts in the early years of the twentieth century. The sleeves are made in plain stockinette stitch to give your hands a rest and to provide a contrast to the all-over dense patterning on the body. The sweater is made from the top down, so you can easily make it longer if you desire. ❧

Sizes
Adult **Small** (Medium, Large)

Finished Measurements
Bust: **34** (38.5, 43)"/86.5 (98, 109)cm
Length: 18 (18.5, 19.5)"/45.5 (47, 49.5)cm

Materials 🧶 2 🧶
◆ Schoolhouse Press *Québécoise*, 100% wool, 3.5oz/100g, 210yds/192m per skein: Gold #14, 7 (7, 8) skeins

◆ Size 4 (3.5mm) 29"/73.5cm or 16"/40.5cm long circular and double-pointed needles or size needed to obtain gauge
◆ Tapestry needle

Gauge
26 sts = 4"/10cm over lattice chart (blocked)
21 sts = 4"/10cm in St st (blocked)
Adjust needle size as necessary to obtain correct gauge.

PATTERN NOTES

Because these twisted st patterns have maneuvers on every row, this sweater is worked in-the-round from the top down. Steeks are used for armhole and neck shaping. The sleeves are picked up at the armholes and worked down to the cuff.

PATTERN STITCHES

Stockinette stitch (in-the-round):

Knit every round.

Garter stitch (in-the-round):

Knit 1 round, purl 1 round.

CHARTS

A: Left Snake
B: Right Snake
C: Left Rope
D: Right Rope
E: Lattice Panel
F: Lattice Cuff

INSTRUCTIONS

Body

CO 7 sts (armhole steek) and place CC marker for beg of rnd in the center having 3 sts on each side, CO 110 (126, 142) sts (back), pm, CO 7 sts (armhole steek) and place CC marker for side seam in the center, having 3 sts on each side, CO 28 sts (shoulder), CO 31 (neck steek), CO 28 (shoulder), pm for beg of rnd.

Note: Set up pats as follows, placing additional markers between charts if desired:

Set-up: K3, p1, k3 (steek, the center purl makes it easier to cut later); Back—0 (8, 16) sts Left Rope, 20 sts Lattice Panel, 8 sts Left Rope, 9 sts Left Snake, 8 sts Left Rope, 20 sts Lattice Panel, 8 sts Right Rope, 9 sts Right Snake, 8 sts Right Rope, 20 sts Lattice Panel, 0 (8, 16) sts Right Rope (110 [126, 142] sts total for Back); k3, p1, k3 (steek); Front—0 (8, 16) sts Left Rope, 20 sts Lattice Panel, k15, p1, k15 sts (neck steek), 20 sts Lattice Panel, 0 (8, 16) sts Right Rope (20 [28, 36] sts in each shoulder).

Work pats as est until piece measures 4"/10cm from CO.

Neck Shaping

Next rnd: Work in pats as est, BO neck steek sts.

Next rnd: Work in pats as est, CO 70 sts for neck.

Next rnd: Work in pats as est, working 70 neck sts as foll: Beg chart row to match with existing ladder and lattice sections—8 sts Left Rope, 9 sts Left Snake, 8 sts Left Rope, 20 sts Lattice Panel, 8 sts Right Rope, 9 sts Right Snake, 8 sts Right Rope.

Note: Front and Back are now the same. Work even until piece measures 8.5 (9, 9.5)"/21.5 (23, 24)cm.

Armhole Shaping

Next rnd: Work pats as est and BO armhole steeks.

Next rnd: Work pats as est and CO 12 sts over each armhole steek.

Next rnd: Work pats as est and p14 sts (12 CO plus existing 2 purl sts outside of steek) at each armhole for gusset.

Dec rnd: Work pats as est and p2tog (first 2 and last 2 sts of armhole gusset).

Rep Dec rnd every other rnd until 2 sts rem in gusset.

Next rnd: Work pats as est and p2tog at underarm. Leave this purl st as a side seam st for remainder of knitting.

Work even until body measures approx 18 (18.5, 19.5)"/45.5 (47, 49.5) cm or desired length. BO.

With sewing machine, sew two rows of straight stitching on either side of center st in each steek. Cut off extra fabric. Sew shoulder seams.

Sleeves

Join yarn at beg of armhole gusset and purl across 12 sts, pick up 90 (94, 98) sts around armhole, p6, pm for beg of rnd—102 (106, 110) sts.

Work in St st (do not twist sts) with purl sts as est for gussets and dec every 6th rnd as foll:

Dec rnd: Work pats as est and p2tog (first 2 and last 2 sts of armhole gusset).

Rep Dec every 4th rnd until 2 sts rem in gusset. Work 3 rnds even.

Next rnd: Work pats as est and p2tog at underarm. **Note:** Leave this purl st as a side seam st for remainder of knitting—91 (95, 99) sts.

Dec every 4th rnd 18 (20, 18) times until 55 (55, 63) sts rem as foll:

Dec rnd: K1, ssk, knit to last 4 sts, k2tog, k1, p1.

Work even until sleeve measures 13"/33cm and dec 1 st on last row—54 (54, 62) sts.

Cuff

Next rnd: P3 (3, 1), work Lattice Cuff Chart rep to last 3 (3, 1) st(s), p3 (3, 1).

Cont to foll Lattice Cuff Chart as est until cuff measures 3"/7.5cm. BO.

Finishing

Sew two rows of machine stitching at outside edge of neck steek near neck opening. Cut off extra fabric.

Neckband

With RS facing, beg at left back shoulder corner, pick up 24 sts down side of neck, pick up 1 st in corner (mark this and all corner sts), pick up 50 sts across front neck, 1 st in corner, 24 sts up other side of neck, 1 st in corner, 50 sts across back neck and 1 st in corner.

Rnd 1: *Purl to corner st, knit corner st; rep from * around.

Rnd 2: *Knit to 1 st before corner st, s2kp (slip 2tog kw, k1, p2sso); rep from * around.

Rep last 2 rnds until neckband measures 1"/2.5cm. BO knitwise.

Weave in ends. Wash and block to measurements.

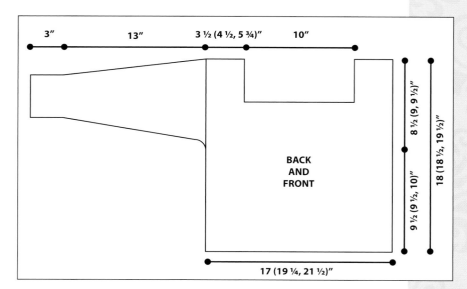

Lattice Panel

20 19 18 17 16 15 14 13 12 11 10 9 8 7 6 5 4 3 2 1

(rows, top to bottom) 23, 22, 21, 20, 19, 18, 17, 16, 15, 14, 13, 12, 11, 10, 9, 8, 7, 6, 5, 4, 3, 2, 1

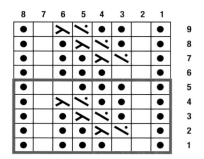

Left Rope

8 7 6 5 4 3 2 1

9, 8, 7, 6, 5, 4, 3, 2, 1

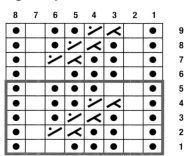

Right Rope

8 7 6 5 4 3 2 1

9, 8, 7, 6, 5, 4, 3, 2, 1

Left Snake

9 8 7 6 5 4 3 2 1

(chart rows 26 down to 1)

Right Snake

9 8 7 6 5 4 3 2 1

(chart rows 26 down to 1)

<table>
<tr><th colspan="10">KEY</th></tr>
<tr><td>•</td><td colspan="9">Purl</td></tr>
<tr><td></td><td colspan="9">Knit</td></tr>
</table>

Right Twist
Skip the first stitch, knit into 2nd stitch, then knit skipped stitch. Slip both stitches from needle together OR k2tog leaving sts on LH needle, then k first st again, sl both sts off needle

Right Twist, purl bg
Sl1 to CN, hold in back. k1, p1 from CN

Left Twist, purl bg
Sl1 to CN, hold in front. p1, k1 from CN

Left Twist
Sl1 to CN left in front. K1, k1 from CN
C2 over 1 left P: sl1 to CN, hold in front. P1, k2 from CN
C2 over 1 left: sl2 to CN, hold in front. K1, k2 from CN
C2 over 1 right p: sl1 to CN, hold in back. K2, p1 from CN
C2 over 1 right: sl1 to CN, hold in back. K2, k1 from CN

Lattice Cuff

12 11 10 9 8 7 6 5 4 3 2 1

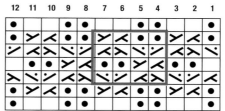

(chart rows 7 down to 1)

BULGARIAN ROSES INTARSIA CARDIGAN

DESIGN BY DONNA DRUCHUNAS

I've always been in love with floral intarsia sweaters, but I've never had the stamina to knit one for myself. Although the pattern is knitted entirely in stockinette stitch, changing colors every few stitches over the entire surface of a sweater always seemed daunting to me. When I saw the intarsia rose motifs on a pair of socks from Bulgaria, I knew I had to put this design onto a cardigan. Instead of covering the whole surface of the sweater with a repeating pattern, I took advantage of the fact that intarsia can be done in isolated areas, and put one large bouquet on the right front, a few flowers on the left shoulder, and one bud on the left sleeve. The border pattern is worked in stranded knitting and the rest of the sweater is knit with just one color. Because it is worked at 4 stitches per inch, this sweater also works up more quickly than you can imagine. ❧

Sizes
Adult **Small** (Medium, Large)

Finished Measurements
Bust: 40 (44, 48)"/101.5 (112, 122)cm
Length: 19 (20, 21)"/48.5 (51, 53.5)cm

Materials
- Blue Sky Alpacas *Worsted Hand Dyes*, 50% Royal alpaca, 50% Merino, 100g/3.5oz, 100yds/91m per skein: Charcoal #2025 (MC), 10 (11, 12) skeins; Ecru #2003 (A), 2 (2, 3) skeins; Petunia #2026 (B), Red #2000 (C), Mulberry #2024 (D), Lagoon #2023 (E), Green #2002 (F), 1 skein each
- Size 9 (5.5mm) needles or size needed to obtain gauge
- Size 7 (4.5mm), 20"/51cm long circular needle
- Tapestry needle
- Seven buttons 1"/2.5cm in diameter

Gauge
16 sts = 4"/10cm in stockinette st on larger needle
Adjust needle size as necessary to obtain correct gauge.

PATTERN STITCHES

Stockinette stitch

Knit RS rows, purl WS rows.

Moss stitch

Worked over an even number of sts.

Row 1 (WS): (K1, p1) across.

Row 2: Knit the knits and purl the purls.

Row 3: (P1, k1) across.

Row 4: Knit the knits and purl the purls.

Rep Rows 1–4 for moss st.

CHARTS

A: Right Front Border (multiple of 6 sts)

B: Left Front Border (multiple of 6 sts)

C: Back Border (multiple of 6 sts)

D: Right Front Bouquet

E: Left Front Rose

F: Sleeve Rosebud

INSTRUCTIONS

Right Front

With smaller needles and A, CO 40 (40, 46) sts.

Work 7 rows in moss st. Change to larger needles.

Next row (RS): Beg working in St st and foll Right Front Border chart, in 0 (4, 2) sts evenly across last row—40 (44, 48) sts.

When all rows of chart are complete, cut A. Work 2 rows of St st in MC only.

Beg working Right Front Bouquet intarsia pat foll chart on center 40 sts and working any extra sts on each side in MC.

When all rows of chart are complete, cont in St st and with MC only.

Work until piece measures 11 (11.5, 12)"/28 (29, 30.5)cm from CO edge, ending after a RS row.

Armhole Shaping

Next row (WS): BO 7 (8, 9) sts at beg of row—33 (36, 39) sts.

Work until armhole measures 8 (8.5, 9)"/20.5 (21.5, 23)cm, ending after a WS row.

Neck Shaping

Next row (RS): BO 7 (8, 9) sts at beg of row—26 (28, 30) sts.

BO 3 sts at beg of next 2 RS rows—20 (22, 24) sts.

Shoulder Shaping

BO 7 (7, 8) sts at beg of next 2 WS rows, then 6 (8, 8) sts at beg of next WS row.

Left Front

Work as for Right Front except foll chart for Left Front Border.

Omit Right Front Bouquet Chart, instead work Left Front Rose Chart on shoulder, beg immediately after armhole shaping is complete.

Armhole Shaping

Next row (RS): BO 7 (8, 9) sts at beg of row—33 (36, 39) sts.

Work until armhole measures 8 (8.5, 9)"/20.5 (21.5, 23)cm, ending after a RS row.

Neck Shaping

Next row (WS): BO 7 (8, 9) sts at beg of row—26 (28, 30) sts.

BO 3 sts at beg of next 2 WS rows—20 (22, 24) sts.

Shoulder Shaping

BO 7 (7, 8) sts at beg of next 2 RS rows, then 6 (8, 8) sts at beg of next RS row.

Back

With smaller needles and A, CO 80 (86, 92) sts.

Work 7 rows in moss st. Change to larger needles.

Next row (RS): Beg working in St st and foll Back Border Chart, inc 0 (2, 4) sts evenly across last row—80 (88, 96) sts.

When all rows of chart are complete, cut A. Work in St st with MC only until piece measures 11 (11.5, 12)"/28.5 (29, 30.5)cm from CO edge, ending after a WS row.

Armhole Shaping

BO 7 (8, 9) sts at beg of 2 rows—66 (72, 78) sts.

Work until piece measures .5"/1.25cm less than fronts at shoulders, ending after a WS row.

Neck Shaping

Next row (RS): BO center 26 (28, 30) sts—20 (22, 24) sts rem in each shoulder.

Shoulder Shaping

Work until piece measures same as fronts at shoulders, then shape shoulders as for fronts, working each separately or both at the same time with two separate balls of yarn.

Left Sleeve

With A and smaller needles, CO 30 sts.

Work 7 rows in moss st. Change to larger needles.

Next row (RS): Beg working in St st and foll Back Border Chart.

When all rows of chart are complete, cut A. Work 2 rows of St st in MC only.

Beg working Right Front Bouquet Chart on center 17 sts and working any sts on each side in MC.

When all rows of chart are complete, cont in St st with MC only until sleeve measures 14.5 (16.5, 18.5)"/37 (42, 47)cm; AT THE SAME TIME, immediately after completing Border Chart, inc 1 st at beg and end of next and every 4th row 16 (18, 20) times—64 (68, 72) sts.

Change to moss st and work 1.25 (1.5, 1.75)"/3 (4, 4.5)cm.

BO.

Right Sleeve

Work same as for Left Sleeve, omitting intarsia motif.

Finishing

Sew shoulder seams. Sew sleeves into armholes. Sew underarm and side seams.

Button Band

With RS facing, smaller needles, and MC, pick up 56 (60, 64) sts along right front edge. Work in moss st for 1"/2.5cm. BO loosely in pat.

Place markers for buttons with first one 1"/2.5cm from bottom and top one to be made in 1"/2.5cm neckband and 5 more evenly spaced between.

Buttonhole Band

With RS facing, smaller needles, and MC, pick up 56 (60, 64) sts along left front edge.

Work in moss st for .5"/1.25cm.

Next row (RS): Work in moss st to next marker, *yo, k2tog or p2tog; rep from * across all markers, work in moss st to end of row.

Left Front Border Chart

Back Border Chart

Right Front Edge Chart

Work in moss st until band measures 1"/2.5cm. BO loosely in pat.

Sew buttons opposite buttonholes.

Neckband

Mark the sts that align with the corners on the back neck shaping.

Work in moss st except at the marked sts; on RS rows work the sts immediately before and after the marked st tog with corner st as foll: sl2-tog-kw, k1, p2sso.

Work until band measures 1"/2.5cm, working 7th buttonhole after .5"/1.25cm.

BO loosely in pat.

Weave in ends. Wash and dry flat to block.

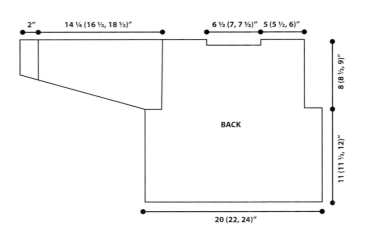

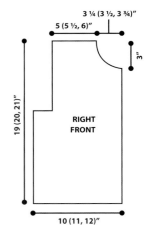

Left Front Rose Chart

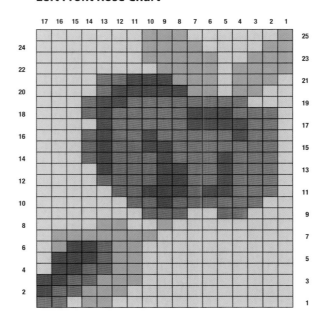

KEY

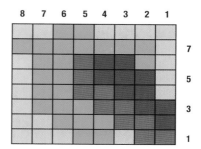

	MC: Charcoal #2025
	A: Ecru #2003
	B: Petunia #2026
	C: Red #2000
	D: Mulberry #2024
	E: Lagoon #2023
	F: Green #2002
	G: Orange #2010

Sleeve Rosebud Chart

Bouquet Right Front

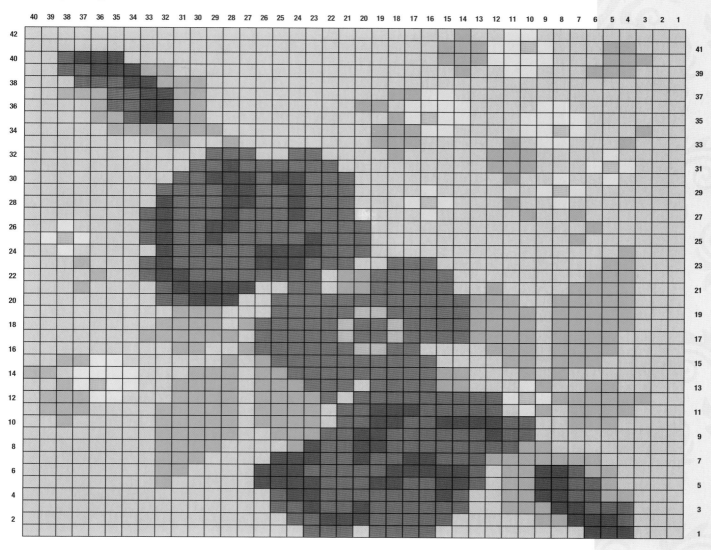

SWEATERS OF THE
UNITED KINGDOM &
IRELAND

ST. OLAF MEN'S FAIR ISLE SWEATER

DESIGN BY CANDACE EISNER STRICK

This sweater is named in honor of St. Olaf Street in downtown Lerwick, Shetland, a lovely, old street lined with houses on one side and a beautiful bowling green and gardens on the other. We stayed in a bed-and-breakfast on this street when we visited Shetland in 1998. It was a short walk to Jamieson & Smith and all of downtown Lerwick. ❧

Sizes
Man's Small (**Medium**, Large)

Finished Measurements
Chest: 40 (**46**, 51.5)"/101.5 (117, 131)cm
Length: 23.5 (24.5, 27.25)"/59.5 (62, 69)cm

Materials ⬛1⬛
◆ Jamieson & Smith *Jumper Weight*, 100% wool, 1oz/25g, 130yds/119m per skein: Dark Brown #5 (A), 9 (10, 11) skeins; Medium Brown #4 (B), 1 (1, 2) skeins; Moorit #2 (C),

Beige #3 (D), and Off White #1A (E), 2 (2, 3) skeins each; Raspberry #133 (F), 5 (5, 6) skeins; Mustard #121 (G), 1 skein
◆ Sizes 2 (2.75mm) and 3 (3.25mm) 24"/61cm and 16"/40.5cm long circular and double-pointed needles or size needed to obtain gauge
◆ Stitch markers
◆ Waste yarn or stitch holders

Gauge
28 sts and 32 rnds = 4"/10cm in St st with size 3 (3.25mm) needles
Adjust needle size as necessary to obtain correct gauge.

INSTRUCTIONS

Body

With smaller circular needle 24"/61cm long and A, CO 256 (296, 336) sts. Pm (first marker) at beg of rnd and join, being careful not to twist sts. Work in k2, p2 ribbing in the foll color/rnd sequence for 27 rnds:

Color/Rnd Sequence:

K2	P2	# of rnds
A	E	2
A	D	3
A	C	3
B	C	4
F	G	3
B	C	4
A	C	3
A	D	3
A	E	2

Knit 1 rnd with A, inc 24 sts evenly spaced—280 (320, 360) sts.

Change to larger circular needle 24"/61cm long. Beg on Rnd 35 (25, 2) of Chart A, working 20-st rep around body 14 (16, 18) times, through Rnd 115.

On Rnd 116 (last rnd of chart), mark for front and back working 140 (160, 180) sts, pm (referred to as 2nd marker), work to first marker.

Divide for Armholes

Beg Chart A again, working 8 (0, 0) rnds.

Foll Rnd 9 (1, 1) of Chart A, work to 3 sts before 2nd marker, place next 7 sts on a holder, pm, CO 11 sts in alternating colors for armhole steek (referred to as second armhole steek), pm, work to 3 sts before first marker, place next 7 sts on a holder, pm, CO 11 sts in alternating colors for armhole steek (referred to as first armhole steek), pm—133 (153, 173) sts.

Note: All rnds now beg and end in middle of first steek. Ends do not need to be worked in anymore, as this steek will be cut and trimmed later on. Work all steeks in alternating colors with the 2 colors used in any one rnd, creating stripes. When the steeks are cut later on, it is easy to see where to cut by following the vertical stripes.

Work in pat as est through Rnd 57, remembering to beg first pat rep for front and back on 5th st from right-hand side of chart.

Front Neck Shaping

Foll Rnd 58, work 54 (62, 72) sts, place center 25 (29, 29) sts on a holder for front neck, pm, CO 11 sts for front neck steek in alternating colors, pm, work rem 54 (62, 72) sts of front, work back sts.

Note: Work front neck steek same as armhole steeks. Decs are worked on each side of front steek as foll: k2tog, work 11 steek sts, ssk.

Beg on next rnd (Rnd 59), dec 1 st each side of neck every other rnd 11 times—43 (51, 61) sts rem for each shoulder.

Work even through Rnd 68 (80, 80).

Back Neck Shaping

Foll Rnd 69 (81, 81), work sts of front, work next 47 (55, 65) sts, place center 39 (43, 43) sts on holder for back neck, pm, CO 11 sts in alternating colors for back neck steek, pm, work rem 47 (55, 65) sts of back.

Note: Back neck steek is worked same as others and decs are worked same as front neck shaping.

Dec 1 st each side of back neck every rnd 4 times.

Next rnd: Work sts of front, BO sts of 2nd armhole steek, work sts of back, BO 11 steek sts of back neck, BO first 6 sts of first armhole steek.

Next rnd: BO rem steek sts of first armhole steek. Work sts of front, BO front neck steek sts. **Note:** Front is worked one more row than back.

Place rem 43 (51, 61) sts of each shoulder on larger dpns.

Machine stitch and cut through center of steeks; join shoulders using 3-needle bind-off method.

Neckband

Note: When picking up sts around neck, use the st that is directly adjacent to first steek st.

Using smaller circular needle, 16"/40.5cm long and A, beg at back right shoulder, pick up and knit 6 sts down right back, k39 (43, 43) sts from back neck holder, pick up and knit 6 sts up left back, pick up and knit 19 (29, 29) sts down left front, k25 (29, 29) sts from front neck holder, pick up and knit 21 (31, 31) sts up right front, pm—116 (144, 144) sts.

Work 1 rnd of k2 A, k2 E, then work in foll rnd/color sequence in k2, p2 rib:

K2	P2	#of rnd.
A	E	2
A	D	3
A	C	3
B	C	1
F	G	2

Work one rnd of p2 F, p2 G for turning rnd (hem).

Hem

Knit 1 rnd with F. Knit 1 rnd with A, dec 16 (20, 20) sts evenly spaced—100 (124, 124) sts. Knit 8 more rnds. Turn back hem on purl line and sew live sts down very loosely.

Sleeves

Note: When picking up sts around sleeve opening, use the st that is directly adjacent to the first steek st. Change to dpns when necessary.

With smaller circular needle, 16"/40.5cm long and A, knit last 3 sts from underarm holder, pick up and knit 67 (87, 87) sts to shoulder seam, pick up and knit 66 (86, 86) sts to holder, k3 sts from holder, pm, knit last st from holder, pm—140 (180, 180) sts.

Note: This marked-off st is now the underarm "seam" st and is always worked in A. All decs are worked on each side of this st as foll: k2tog, knit to within 2 sts of marker, ssk.

Beg Chart B on Rnd 11 (1, 1), dec 1 st each side of marker every 2nd rnd 15 (20, 20) times, then every 3rd rnd 20 (25, 25) times—70 (90, 90) sts. Work even through Rnd 114 (125, 125).

Knit 1 rnd with A, dec 14 sts evenly spaced—56 (76, 76) sts.

Change to smaller dpns and work ribbing in same color/rnd sequence as for body. Loosely BO in knit using A.

Finishing

Trim and finish steeks. Weave in any loose ends.

Steam lightly or wash and dry on a wooly board.

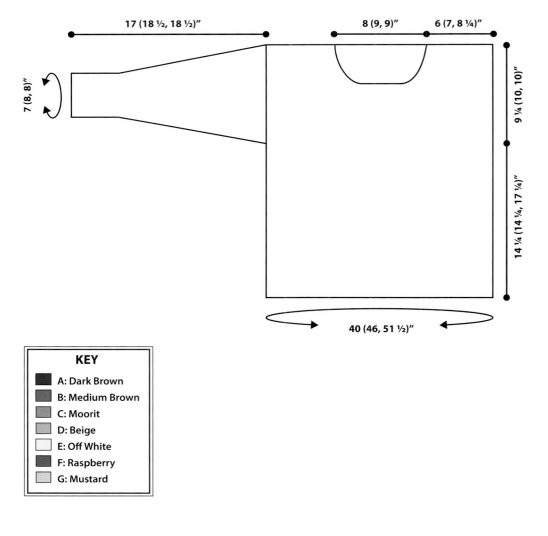

17 (18 ½, 18 ½)"   8 (9, 9)"   6 (7, 8 ¼)"

7 (8, 8)"

9 ¼ (10, 10)"

14 ¼ (14 ¼, 17 ¼)"

40 (46, 51 ½)"

KEY

- ■ A: Dark Brown
- ■ B: Medium Brown
- ■ C: Moorit
- ■ D: Beige
- □ E: Off White
- ■ F: Raspberry
- ■ G: Mustard

Chart A

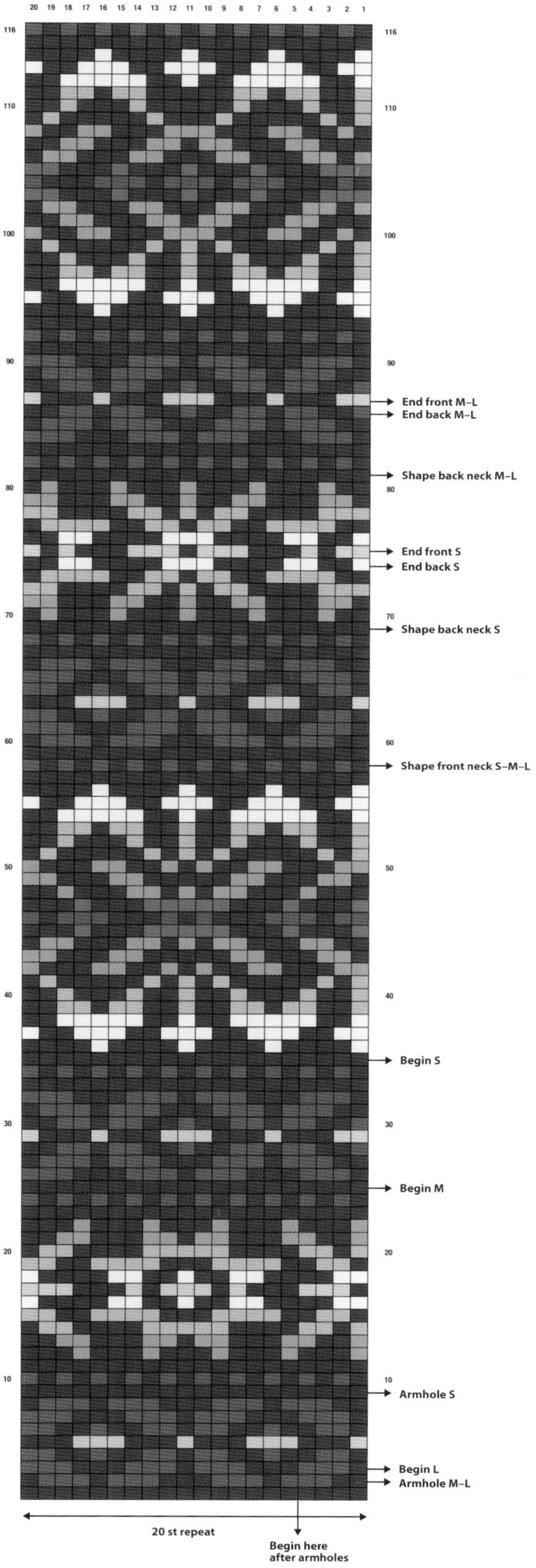

20 19 18 17 16 15 14 13 12 11 10 9 8 7 6 5 4 3 2 1
116
110
100
90
80
70
60
50
40
30
20
10
End front M–L
End back M–L
Shape back neck M–L
End front S
End back S
Shape back neck S
Shape front neck S–M–L
Begin S
Begin M
Armhole S
Begin L
Armhole M–L
20 st repeat
Begin here after armholes

Chart B

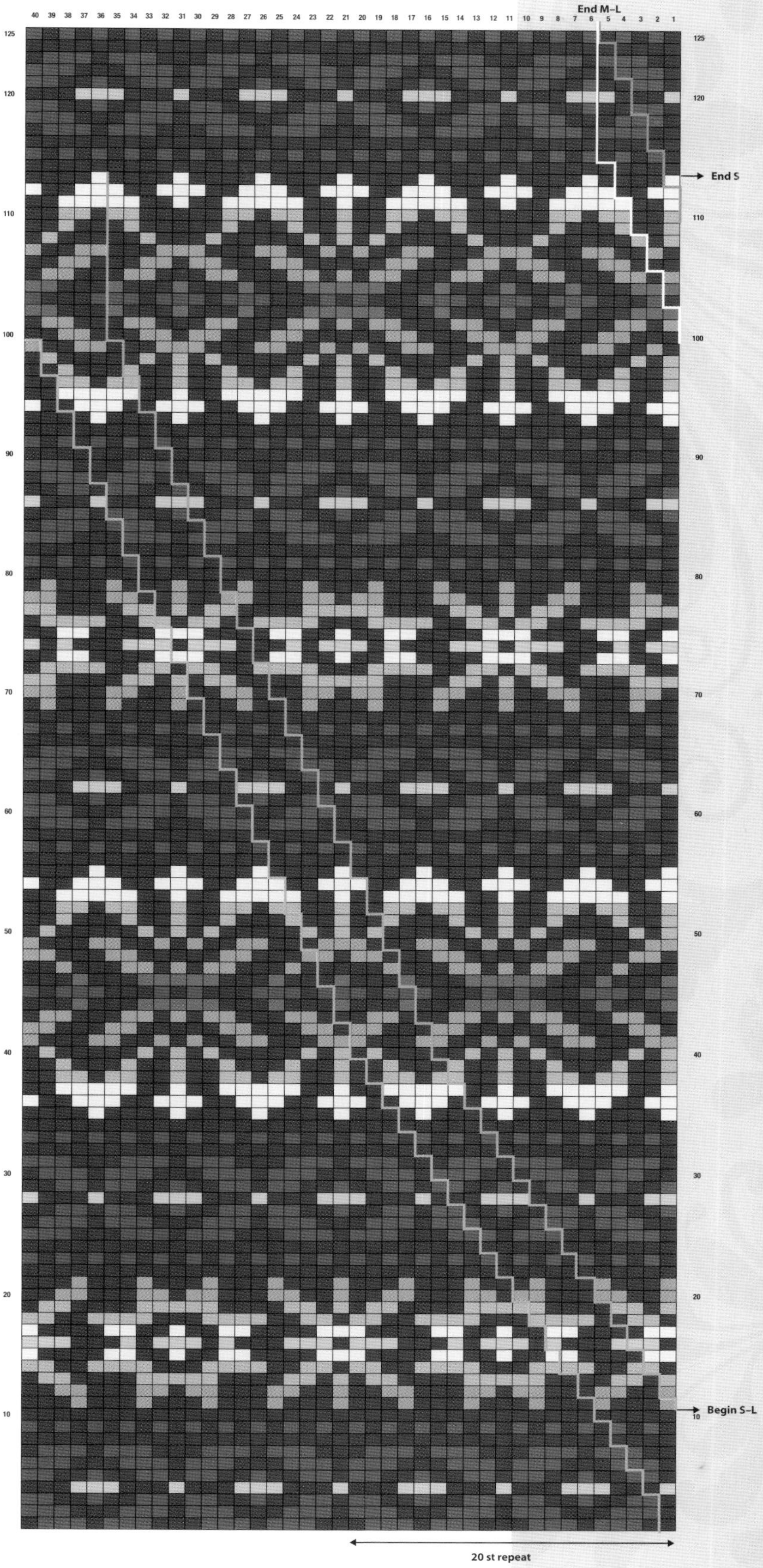

End M–L
40 39 38 37 36 35 34 33 32 31 30 29 28 27 26 25 24 23 22 21 20 19 18 17 16 15 14 13 12 11 10 9 8 7 6 5 4 3 2 1
125
120
110
100
90
80
70
60
50
40
30
20
10
End S
Begin S–L
20 st repeat

LEVENWICK FAIR ISLE JACKET

DESIGN BY MELISSA LEAPMAN

Flaunt your stranded knitting prowess by knitting this design. It uses traditional Fair Isle techniques, including steeks, to create a showstopper cardigan jacket. Although the colorwork looks very complicated, only two colors are worked per row! ❧

Sizes

Adult Small (**Medium**, Large, XLarge, XXLarge)

Finished Measurements

Bust (buttoned): 34.5 (**38.5**, 42.5, 46.5, 50.5)"/87.5 (98, 108, 118, 128.5)cm

Length: 24.5 (24.75, 25, 25.5, 26)"/62 (63, 63.5, 65, 66)cm

Materials (4)

◆ Cascade 220, 100% wool, 100g/3.5oz, 220yds/209m per skein: Eggplant #8418 (A), 3 (4, 4, 5, 5) skeins; Persimmon #4146 (B), Zinia #9466 (C), Ruby #9404 (D), and Burgundy #2401 (E), 1 (1, 2, 2, 2) skeins each

◆ Size 6 (4mm) 24"/61cm and 29"/73.5cm long circular knitting needle

◆ Size 8 (5mm) 16"/40.5cm, 24"/61cm, and 29"/73.5cm long circular knitting needles or size needed to obtain gauge

◆ Sizes 6 (4mm) and 8 (5mm) double-pointed needles

◆ Optional: One size F/5 (3.75mm) crochet hook for crocheted steek

◆ Stitch markers (one in contrasting color to mark beg of rnds)

◆ Tapestry needle

◆ 4 buttons (JHB International's Shell Spin #70326 was used on sample garment)

Gauge

20 sts and 20 rnds = 4"/10cm in Fair Isle pat with larger circular needle

Adjust needle size as necessary to obtain correct gauge.

PATTERN NOTES

This design is worked entirely in-the-round from the bottom up, using steeks for the front opening, the armholes, and the neck opening; the set-in sleeves are worked in-the-round separately from the body, using steeks to shape the sleeve cap.

In chart, background color is the color used the most on that particular round.

Stripe pattern for steeks: For 5-stitch steeks, work (k1 background color, k1 contrast color) twice, k1 background color.

When casting on for steeks, use e-wrap cast-on technique, alternating colors to match steek stripe pattern.

To increase within pattern, use the M1 knitwise technique in the color needed to maintain the Fair Isle pattern.

CHARTS

Border Pattern Knitted In-the-Round (multiple of 4 sts)

Border Pattern Knitted Flat (multiple of 4 sts)

Colorwork Pattern

INSTRUCTIONS

Body

With smaller circular needle and A, CO 145 (161, 181, 197, 213) sts.

Set-up: Work 5 sts in stripe pat for steeks, pm for beg of rnd, work Rnd 1 of Border Pat across next 140 (156, 176, 192, 208) sts, pm for end of rnd.

Cont even until Rnd 11 of Border Pat is completed, inc 25 (29, 29, 33, 37) sts evenly between beg of rnd marker and end of rnd marker along last rnd—170 (190, 210, 230, 250) sts.

Change to larger circular needle.

Next rnd: With A, work first 5 sts in stripe pat for steek (see Pattern Notes), sm, k39 (44, 49, 54, 59), pm, k87 (97, 107, 117, 127), pm, k39 (44, 49, 54, 59), sm.

Next rnd: Work 5 sts in stripe pat for steek, sm, work Rnd 1 of Colorwork Pat around.

Cont even in est pats until piece measures approx 17"/43cm from beg, ending after pat Rnd 34.

Divide for Armholes

Next rnd: Work pats as est until 5 (6, 7, 9, 11) sts before next marker, break CC (contrast color), remove marker, BO next 10 (12, 14, 18, 22) sts with background color, rejoin CC, work pats as est across to 5 (6, 7, 9, 11) sts before next marker, break CC, remove marker, BO next 10 (12, 14, 18, 22) sts with background color, rejoin CC, work pats as est across to end of rnd marker.

Next rnd: Work pats as est until first armhole, CO 5 sts for armhole steek, work pats as est across to next set of BO sts, CO 5 sts for armhole steek, pm, work pats as est across to end rnd.

Dec rnd: Work pats as est until 2 sts before 2nd marker, k2tog, sm, work 5 sts in stripe pat for steek (see Pattern Notes), sm, ssk, work pats as est across until 2 sts before next marker, k2tog, work 5 sts in stripe pat for steek (see Pattern Notes), sm, ssk, work pats as est across to end row.

Rep Dec rnd every rnd 0 (1, 5, 8, 10) times, every other rnd 4 (7, 6, 5, 5) times, then every 4th rnd 1 (0, 0, 0, 0) times.

Cont even in est pats until piece measures approx 22 (22.25, 22.5, 23, 23.5)"/56 (56.5, 57, 58.5, 59.5)cm from beg, ending 6 sts before end of rnd marker. Break CC.

Front Neck Shaping

Next rnd: BO 17 sts with background color, rejoin CC, cont pats as est across to end of rnd marker.

Next rnd: CO 5 sts for front neck steek, pm for beg of rnd, work pats as est across to end of rnd marker.

Dec rnd: Work 5 sts in stripe pat for steek (see Pattern Notes), sm, ssk, cont pats as est across until 2 sts before end of rnd marker, k2tog.

Rep Dec rnd once more, then every other rnd 4 times.

Cont even in pats as est until piece measures approx 24 (24.25, 24.5, 25, 25.5)"/61 (61.5, 62, 63.5, 65)cm from beg.

Back Neck Shaping

Next rnd: Work across to next marker, cont pats as est across next 18 (19, 20, 21, 22) sts, BO next 29 sts, cont across to end rnd.

Next rnd: Work across BO back neck sts, pm, CO 5 sts for back neck steek, pm, cont across to end rnd.

Dec rnd: Work across until 2 sts before back steek sts, k2tog, sm, work 5 sts in stripe pat for back neck steek (see Pattern Notes), sm, ssk, cont across to end rnd.

Rep Dec rnd once more.

Cont even in est pats until piece measures approx 24.5 (24.75, 25, 25.5, 26)"/62 (63, 63.5, 65, 66)cm from beg.

BO all sts using background color.

Sleeves

With smaller dpns and A, CO 80 (80, 84, 88, 92) sts. Pm at beg of rnd and join, being careful not to twists sts.

Beg Border Pat, and cont even until Rnd 11 is completed, inc 1 st at beg of last rnd—81 (81, 85, 89, 93) sts.

Change to larger dpns.

Work Rnd 1 of Colorwork Pat around.

Dec rnd: K1, k2tog, work pat as est across to 2 sts before next marker, ssk, work next st in pat as est.

Rep Dec rnd every other rnd 1 (0, 0, 0, 0) times, every 4th rnd 6 (0, 0, 0, 0) times, every 6th rnd 0 (4, 4, 1, 1) times, then every 8th rnd 0 (0, 0, 2, 2) times—65 (71, 75, 81, 85) sts rem.

Cont even in est pats until piece measures approx 9"/23cm from beg, ending after same pat rnd as the body at armholes, ending 5 (6, 7, 9, 11) sts before end of rnd marker.

Cap Shaping

BO next 10 (12, 14, 18, 22) sts, work pat as est across to end rnd.

Next rnd: CO 5 sts for sleeve cap steek, pm, work pat as est across to end rnd.

Dec rnd: Work first 5 sts in stripe pat for steek (see Pattern Notes), k2tog, cont pats as est across to within last 2 sts in rnd, ssk.

Rep Dec rnd every other rnd 10 (8, 9, 10, 12) times, then every rnd 6 (10, 9, 9, 7) times—21 (21, 23, 23, 23) sts rem.

BO all sts with background color.

Finishing

Machine stitch back neck, front neck, and armhole steeks and cut through center of steeks. Using mattress stitch, sew shoulder seams.

Neckband

With RS facing, smaller circular needle, and A, pick up and knit 80 sts along neckline.

Next row (WS): With A, purl across.

Beg Border Pat (knitted flat) and cont even until Row 11 is completed.

BO all sts with A.

Button Band

With RS facing, smaller circular needle, and A, pick up and knit 100 (100, 104, 104, 108) sts along left front edge, including side of neckband.

Beg Border Pat (knitted flat) and cont even until Row 11 is completed.

BO all sts with A.

Place markers for 4 buttons, with the first one .75"/1cm from the top edge, the 4th one 12"/30.5cm from top edge, and the others evenly spaced between.

Buttonhole Band

With RS facing, smaller circular needle, and A, pick up and knit 100 (100, 104, 104, 108) sts along left front edge, including side of neckband.

Complete same as button band working buttonholes opposite markers (BO 3 sts for each buttonhole and on subsequent row, CO 3 sts over BO sts).

Edging for Front Bands

With RS facing, smaller needles, and A, pick up and knit 100 (100, 104, 104, 108) sts along top of right front band.

Next row (WS): Knit as you BO.

Rep this edging along top edge of left front band and along bottom edge of both right and left front bands.

Set in Sleeves. Sew Sleeve and side seams. Sew on buttons.

Weave in ends.

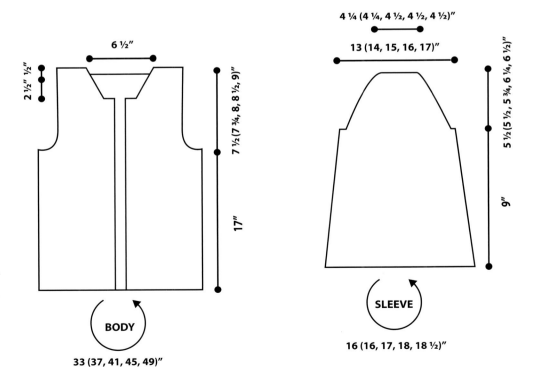

Note: Measurements in schematic illustrations are finished measurements, not including steek stitches or front borders.

Colorwork Pattern

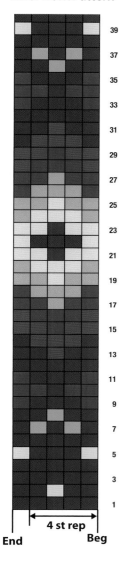

4 st rep

End   Beg

Border Pattern Knitted In-the-Round

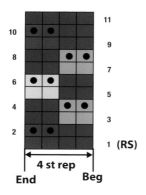

4 st rep

End   Beg

Note: On Rnds 2, 4, 6, 8, and 10 only: Purl sts worked in colors B, C, and D; knit sts worked in color A.

Border Pattern Knitted Flat

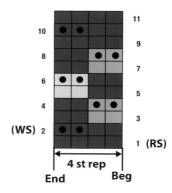

4 st rep

End   Beg

Note: On Rows 2, 4, 6, 8 and 10 only: Knit sts worked in colors B, C, and D; Purl sts worked in color A.

KEY

A: Eggplant #8418
B: Persimmon #4146
C: Zinia #9466
D: Ruby #9404
E: Burgundy #2401
K on RS rows/rnds; p on WS rows
● K on WS rows

KINLOCH ARAN PULLOVER

DESIGN BY MELISSA LEAPMAN

Here's a Celtic winter warmer that showcases Aran cables. Strategically placed increases and decreases are used in the center panel design to accommodate the cabled sections, which appear to come out of nowhere. This sweater is definitely fun to knit! ✎

Sizes
Adult Small (**Medium**, Large, XLarge, XXLarge)

Finished Measurements
Bust: 35 (**40**, 45, 50, 54.5)"/89 (101.5, 114.5, 137, 138.5)cm
Total length: 22.25"/56.5cm

Materials
- Cascade Yarns *Lana D'Oro*, 50% alpaca/50% wool, 100g/3.5oz, 219yds/200m per skein: #1090 Harvest Orange, 6 (7, 8, 8) skeins

- Sizes 5 (3.75mm) and 7 (4.50mm) needles or size needed to obtain gauge
- Two cable needles
- Tapestry needle

Gauge
20 sts and 28 rows = 4"/10cm in Double Seed St with larger needles
Cable Panel A = 2"/5cm wide
Cable Panel B = 5"/12.5cm wide
Adjust needle size as necessary to obtain correct gauge.

STITCH PATTERNS

K2, P2 Rib Pattern (multiple 4 + 2 sts):

Row 1 (RS): *P2, k2; rep from * across, ending with p2.

Row 2: *K2, p2; rep from * across, ending with k2.

Rep Rows 1 and 2 for k2, p2 rib pat.

CHARTS

Double Seed St Pattern (multiple 2 + 1 sts)

Cable Panel A (18 sts)

Cable Panel B (32 sts inc to 44 sts)

INSTRUCTIONS

Back

With smaller needles, CO 90 (102, 114, 126, 138) sts.

Work in k2, p2 rib until piece measures 2"/5cm from beg, ending after RS row.

Next Row (WS): Maintaining est rib pat throughout, work first 7 (13, 19, 25, 31) sts, M1, work next 2 sts, M1, work next 8 sts, M1, work next 21 sts, M1, work next 2 sts, [M1, work rib pat as est in next st] twice, M1, work next 6 sts, [M1, work rib pat as est in next st] twice, M1, work next 2 sts, M1, work next 16 sts, M1, work next 2 sts, M1, work next 8 sts, M1, work next 12 (18, 24, 30, 36) sts to end the row—104 (116, 128, 140, 152) sts. Change to larger needles.

Set-up Pats

Next Row (RS): Work Row 1 of Double Seed St across first 7 (13, 19, 25, 31) sts, Row 1 of Cable Panel A across next 18 sts, Row 1 of Double Seed St across next 11 sts, Row 1 of Cable Panel B across next 32 sts, Row 1 of Double Seed St across next 11 sts, Row 1 of Cable Panel A across next 18 sts, Row 1 of Double Seed St across next 7 (13, 19, 26, 31) sts to end row—104 (116, 128, 140, 152) sts.

Cont pats as est inc 1 st each side every 16th row 4 times—112 (124, 136, 148, 160) sts.

Cont even as est until piece measures approx 14.25 (13.75, 13.25, 13.25, 12.75)"/36 (35, 33.5, 33.5, 32.5)cm from beg, ending after WS row.

Armhole Shaping

BO 4 (5, 6, 7, 8) sts at beg of next 2 rows, then BO 2 (2, 3, 3, 4) sts at beg of next 2 rows. Dec 1 st each side every row 0 (4, 8, 12, 14) times, every other row 2 (5, 4, 3, 3) times, then every 4th row 2 (0, 0, 0, 0) times—92 (92, 94, 95, 102) sts.

Cont even until piece measures 21.25"/54cm from beg, ending after WS row.

Shoulder Shaping

BO 6 (6, 7, 7, 8) sts at beg of next 6 rows, then BO 7 (7, 5, 7, 6) sts at beg of next 2 rows.

BO rem 42 sts.

Front

Work same as Back until piece measures 19.25"/49cm from beg, ending after Row 24 of Cable Panel B.

Neck Shaping

Next Row (RS): Cont in est pats, work across first 36 (36, 37, 39, 41) sts, join 2nd ball of yarn and BO center 20 sts, work across to end row.

Working both sides at once with separate balls of yarn and cont pats as est, BO 6 sts each neck edge once, BO 3 sts each neck edge once, then dec 1 st each neck edge every row twice—25 (25, 26, 28, 30) sts rem each side.

Cont even, if necessary, until piece measures same as Back to shoulders.

Shoulder Shaping

Bind off at each shoulder edge 6 (6, 7, 7, 8) sts 3 times, then 7 (7, 5, 7, 6) sts once.

Sleeves

With smaller needles, CO 54 sts.

Work in k2, p2 rib until piece measures 2"/5cm from beg inc 2 sts on last row, ending after WS row—56 sts. Change to larger needles.

Set-up Pats

Next Row (RS): Work Row 1 of Double Seed St over first 19 sts, Row 1 of Cable Panel A over next 18 sts, Row 1 of Double Seed St over next 19 sts to end row.

Cont pats as est, inc 1 st each side every 6th row 0 (0, 0, 2, 10) times, every 8th row 0 (0, 6, 12, 6) times, every 10th row 0 (6, 6, 0, 0) times, every 12th row 2 (4, 0, 0, 0) times, then every 14th row 6 (0, 0, 0, 0) times, working new sts in Double Seed St pat as they accumulate—72 (76, 80, 84, 88) sts.

Cont even until sleeve measures approx 18.5"/47cm from beg, ending after a WS row.

Cap Shaping

BO 4 (5, 6, 7, 8) sts at beg of next 2 rows. Dec 1 st each side every 4th row 0 (1, 2, 1, 1) times, then every other row 12 (12, 12, 14, 15) times—40 sts rem.

Work 1 (0, 0, 0, 1) row even.

BO 3 sts at beg of next 4 rows.

BO rem 28 sts.

Finishing

Sew right shoulder seam.

Neckband

With RS facing and smaller needles, pick up and knit approx 76 sts along neckline. Work in k2, p2 rib until neckband measures approx 4"/10cm from beg.

BO in pat.

Sew left shoulder seam, including side of neckband.

Set in sleeves. Sew sleeve and side seams.

Weave in ends.

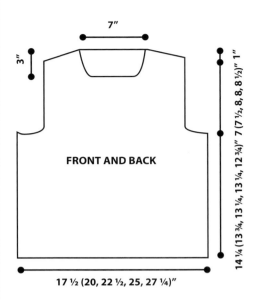

7"

3"

FRONT AND BACK

14 ¼ (13 ¾, 13 ¼, 13 ¼, 12 ¾)" 7 (7 ½, 8, 8, 8 ½)" 1"

17 ½ (20, 22 ½, 25, 27 ¼)"

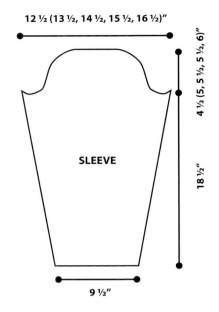

12 ½ (13 ½, 14 ½, 15 ½, 16 ½)"

4 ½ (5, 5 ½, 5 ½, 6)"

18 ½"

SLEEVE

9 ½"

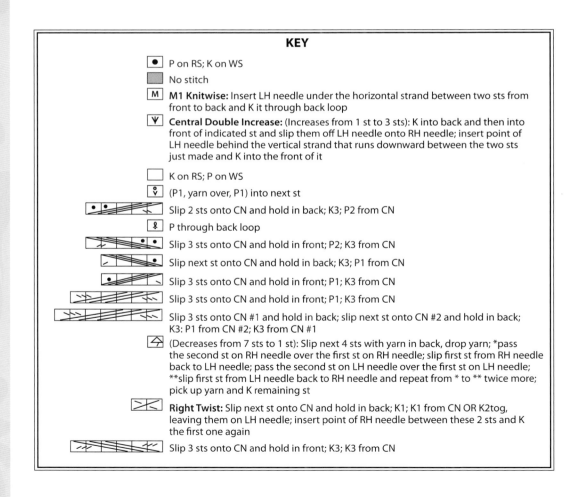

KEY

•	P on RS; K on WS
▨	No stitch
M	**M1 Knitwise:** Insert LH needle under the horizontal strand between two sts from front to back and K it through back loop
⋎	**Central Double Increase:** (Increases from 1 st to 3 sts): K into back and then into front of indicated st and slip them off LH needle onto RH needle; insert point of LH needle behind the vertical strand that runs downward between the two sts just made and K into the front of it
☐	K on RS; P on WS
⋎	(P1, yarn over, P1) into next st
	Slip 2 sts onto CN and hold in back; K3; P2 from CN
ℓ	P through back loop
	Slip 3 sts onto CN and hold in front; P2; K3 from CN
	Slip next st onto CN and hold in back; K3; P1 from CN
	Slip 3 sts onto CN and hold in front; P1; K3 from CN
	Slip 3 sts onto CN and hold in front; P1; K3 from CN
	Slip 3 sts onto CN #1 and hold in back; slip next st onto CN #2 and hold in back; K3: P1 from CN #2; K3 from CN #1
◿	(Decreases from 7 sts to 1 st): Slip next 4 sts with yarn in back, drop yarn; *pass the second st on RH needle over the first st on RH needle; slip first st from RH needle back to LH needle; pass the second st on LH needle over the first st on LH needle; **slip first st from LH needle back to RH needle and repeat from * to ** twice more; pick up yarn and K remaining st
	Right Twist: Slip next st onto CN and hold in back; K1; K1 from CN OR K2tog, leaving them on LH needle; insert point of RH needle between these 2 sts and K the first one again
	Slip 3 sts onto CN and hold in front; K3; K3 from CN

Cable Panel B

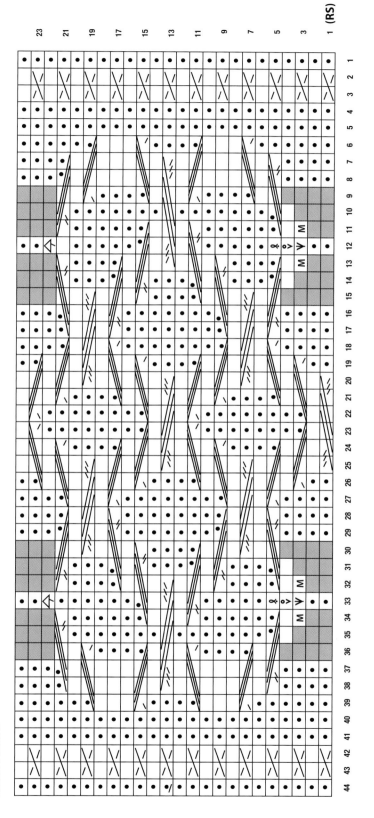

Double Seed Stitch Pattern

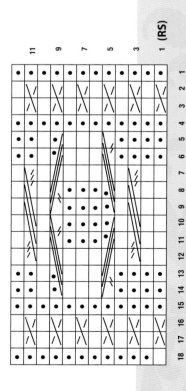

Cable Panel A

ERISKAY GANSEY

DESIGN BY BETH BROWN-REINSEL

This gansey is dedicated to my friend Susan and is my interpretation of a Scottish Eriskay gansey from Rae Compton's book *The Complete Book of Traditional Guernsey and Jersey Knitting* (Arco Publishing, 1985). The name *Eirisgeidh*, or Eriskay, is derived from the Norse for Eric's Isle, located in the Outer Hebrides of Scotland. Many place names on the Island and elsewhere in Scotland are Norse in origin because of the 400 years of Norse occupation (circa AD 800 to 1200). The traditional techniques included in the garment are the Channel Island Cast-On, circular construction, Initials, the Perpendicular Shoulder Join, and Shoulder Strap Neck Gussets. Optional Short Row Shaping is included for adding a little length to the back ❧

Sizes
Adult Small (**Medium**, Large, XLarge, XXLarge)

Finished Measurements
Chest: 36 (**40**, 44, 48, 52)"/ 91.5 (101.5, 112, 122, 132)cm
Length: 22 (23, 24, 25, 26)"/56 (58.5, 61, 63.5, 66)cm

Materials
◆ Louet *Gems Merino*, 100g/3.5oz, 225yds/206m per skein: #43 Pewter, 8 (8, 9, 11, 12) skeins

◆ Size 3 (3.25mm) 16"/40.5cm and 32"/81.5cm long circular and double-pointed needles or size needed to obtain gauge
◆ Stitch markers
◆ Cable needle
◆ Waste yarn or stitch holders
◆ Tapestry needle

Gauge
27 sts and 40 rnds = 4"/10cm in St st
Adjust needle size as necessary to obtain correct gauge.

SPECIAL ABBREVIATIONS

Inc 1L: Increase 1 Left: Pick up bar between 2 sts from front to back and knit into the back.

Inc 1R: Increase 1 Right: pick up bar between 2 sts from back to front and knit into the front.

C2B: K2tog but don't drop sts from left needle, knit first st again, then drop both sts from left needle.

C4B: Slip 2 sts to cn and hold in back, k2, k2 from cn.

C6B: Slip 3 sts to cn and hold in back, k3, k3 from cn.

C8B: Slip 4 sts to cn and hold in back, k4, k4 from cn.

PATTERN NOTES

This gansey is worked flat for the garter st welts at the beginning of the garment. They are then joined and worked in-the-round to the midpoint of the underarm gussets. The body is then split and the front and back are worked separately, flat. The shoulders are joined with a short-row technique called the Perpendicular Shoulder Join. This strap also has gussets. The sleeves are picked up around the armholes and knitted in-the-round to the cuffs. The neck is knitted in-the-round.

Length can be adjusted by knitting more or fewer rows in the Plain Areas of the body and sleeves.

INSTRUCTIONS

Lower Body—Garter Welts (make 2)

Note: These welts (one for the Front and one for the Back) are worked flat and then joined in-the-round.

Using the Channel Island cast-on and shorter circular needle, CO 115 (129, 143, 157, 169) sts.

Rows 1–17: Knit.

Set aside, breaking yarn for the first welt, but not the 2nd welt. Rep using longer circular needle. **Note:** The RS of each welt has 9 purl ridges.

Joining the Welts In-the-Round

Note: As the 2 welts are joined together, 2 seam sts at each side will be est indicated by st markers on each side.

Row 18 (RS): Using longer circular needle, knit across garter welt up to the last st, pm, k1, join to the welt made on the shorter circular needle by knitting 1 st, pm, (the 2 sts between the markers indicate the midpoint of the rnd), knit across welt made on the shorter circular needle up to the last st, pm for beg of rnd, p2, pm—230 (258, 286, 314, 338) sts.

Note: The beg of the rnd is the left side seam, as if you are wearing the gansey. Set the shorter circular needle aside.

Plain Area

Note: The Plain Area is where lengthening or shortening of the entire garment is most easily accomplished. It also creates a smooth surface as a background for the intended wearer's initials.

Rnd 1: Knit, inc 12 sts evenly and working seam st pat (**Note:** First 2 seam sts of Rnd 1 have already been worked; these 2 sts at beg and midpoint will be maintained in this pat until they are put on holders with gusset)—242 (270, 298, 326, 350) sts.

(See Key 1 and Seam St Pat.)

Rnds 2 and 3: Knit, maintaining seam st pat.

Knitting Initials

Chart your initials here. Depending on the width of your letters, they may not all fit in this space.

(See 11-Row Alphabet for Initials Chart).

Rnds 4–14: Work your chosen letters if desired, beg with the 8th st of the front. Knit all other sts while maintaining the seam sts in pat.

Cont to work in-the-round, maintaining the garter seam sts until piece measures 3 (4, 5, 6, 7)"/7.5 (10, 12.5, 15, 18)cm from CO edge.

Optional Short Rows for Back

Because ganseys were rectangular in shape, there was no shaping for the back neck, which can cause the bottom edge to "hike up." If you like, you can add a few sets of short rows in the Plain Area to offset this as foll:

Knit across back to 3 sts before seam sts. Wrap and turn: bring yarn forward, slip next st, take yarn to back and turn work so WS is facing you. Purl across to 3 sts before seam sts, wrap and turn again. Now, knit across entire back, knitting the wrap tog with the st it encircles. Two extra rows have been added in the back. You can work the other wrap together with the adjacent st when you pass it on the next rnd. This short-row shaping can be worked one or two times more if you desire.

Definition Ridge

Note: This element provides a visual base for the patterning.

Work in garter st for 10 rnds as foll:

Rnds 1, 3, 5, 7, 9: Purl, maintaining seam sts in pat.

Rnds 2, 4, 6, 8, 10: Knit, maintaining seam sts in pat.

Patterning

Note: When working Cable pats, note the incs on the set-up rnd only are as foll:

Cable 2 begins with 5 sts + 1 inc = 6 sts.

Cable 4 begins with 6 sts + 2 sts = 8 sts.

Cable 6 begins with 8 sts + 2 sts = 10 sts.

Cable 8 begins with 9 sts + 3 sts = 12 sts.

Set-up rnd: *Work seam sts; Chart A for your size inc'ing 1 (1, 0, 0, 0) st(s); Cable 2 (Cable 2, Cable 4, Cable 6, Cable 8); Chart B; Cable 2 (Cable 2, Cable 4, Cable 6, Cable 8); Chart C; Cable 2 (Cable 2, Cable 4, Cable 6, Cable 8); Chart D; Cable 2 (Cable 2, Cable 4, Cable 6, Cable 8); Chart E; Cable 2 (Cable 2, Cable 4, Cable 6, Cable 8); Chart B; Cable 2 (Cable 2, Cable 4, Cable 6, Cable 8); Chart A for your size inc'ing 1 (1, 0, 0, 0) st(s); rep from * for back.

See Chart A for all sizes

Size Small: 3 sts

Size Medum: 10 sts

Size Large: 13 sts

Size XLarge: 14 sts

Size XXLarge: 17 sts

See Insert Cable Charts (Cable 2, 4, 6, 8)

Cable 2: 6 sts

Cable 4: 8 sts

Cable 6: 10 sts

Cable 8: 12 sts

See Chart E: 11 sts

See Chart C: 11 sts

See Chart D: 21 sts

See Chart B: 21 sts

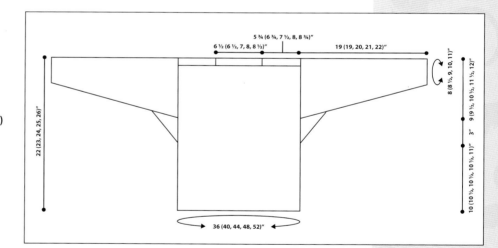

Total sts after Set-up rnd—258 (286, 322, 350, 386) sts. Cont in est pat until piece measures approx 10 (10.5, 10.5, 10.5, 11)"/25.5 (26.5, 26.5, 26.5, 28)cm from CO edge.

Underarm Gusset

Rnd 1: *Work seam st, gusset (Inc 1R), seam st, work across front; rep from * for back.

Rnd 2: *Work seam st, gusset (k1), seam st, work across front; rep from * for back.

Rnd 3: *Work seam st, gusset (Inc 1R, k1, Inc 1L), seam st, work across front; rep from * for back.

Rnds 4 and 5: *Work seam st, gusset (k3), seam st, work across front; rep from * for back.

Rnd 6: *Work seam st, gusset (k1, Inc 1R, k1, Inc 1L, k1), seam st, work across front; rep from * for back.

Cont inc'ing as shown on Gusset Chart every 3rd rnd through Rnd 31 of chart. Put gussets and seam sts (23 sts total) on waste yarn, body is now divided for front and back.

See Key 2

See Lower Gusset Chart

Upper Body

Note: Total sts for each side—127 (141, 159, 173, 191) sts. The front will be worked back and forth to completion before working the back. If you find that a cable row is to be worked on the WS, you can break the yarn and attach it to the other side of the work so that the cables can be crossed on the RS.

Cont working on front charts for a total of 177 rnds, dec'ing 1 (1, 2, 2, 3) sts at the top of each cable in the last rnd—121 (135, 147, 161, 173) sts. Place front sts on waste yarn. Work back as for front.

Shoulder Straps

Note: This area of construction is called a Perpendicular Shoulder Join and involves creating a piece of fabric—the shoulder strap—while joining it to the front and back by means of short rows. This technique is similar to that of turning the heel of a sock. Extra sts to each side of the strap create strap gussets that slope the shoulders.

Right Shoulder

With dpns, CO 25 sts.

Put 37 (44, 48, 51, 55) sts from the front right shoulder and 37 (44, 48, 51, 55) sts from the back right shoulder onto 2 dpn or circular needles. Hold front right shoulder needle in your left hand and the newly CO sts in your right hand (drop back right shoulder needle for the moment).

**Making sure the RS (outside) of sweater is facing you, k1 from the neck edge of left needle and pass last CO st over. Turn work.

Work Rows 1–15 of strap gusset chart or work written instructions as foll:

Row 1 (WS): Slip 1 pwise wyif, p15, k1, p7, p 1 st tog with 1 st from neck edge of other shoulder needle, being careful not to twist shoulder. Turn.

Row 2 (RS): Slip 1 pwise wyib, k4, k2tog, k1, p2, k8, ssk, k4, ssk (using 1 strap st and 1 shoulder st), turn—23 strap sts.

Row 3 (WS): Slip 1 pwise wyif, p12, k2, p7, p2tog, turn.

Row 4 (RS): Slip 1 pwise wyib, k3, k2tog, k3, p2, k6, ssk, k3, ssk, turn—21 strap sts.

Row 5: Slip 1 pwise wyif, p9, k2, p8, p2tog, turn.

Row 6: Slip 1 pwise wyib, k2, k2tog, k5, p2, k4, ssk, k2, ssk, turn—19 strap sts.

Row 7: Slip 1 pwise wyif, p6, k2, p9, p2tog, turn.

Row 8: Slip 1 pwise wyib, k1, k2tog, k7, p2, k2, ssk, k1, ssk, turn—17 strap sts.

Row 9: Slip 1 pwise wyif, p3, k2, p10, p2tog, turn.

Row 10: Slip 1 pwise wyib, k2tog, k9, p1, k1, ssk, ssk, turn—15 strap sts.

Row 11: Slip 1 pwise wyif, p2, k2, p9, p2tog, turn.

Row 12: Slip 1 pwise wyib, k8, p2, k2, slip 1 kwise, slip another kwise, k1, p2sso, turn—14 strap sts.

See Strap Key and Key 1.

See Strap Gusset Chart.

Row 13: Slip 1 pwise wyif, p3, k2, p6, p3tog, turn—13 strap sts.

Row 14: Slip 1 pwise wyib, k5, p2, k4, ssk, turn.

Row 15: Slip 1 pwise wyif, p5, k2, p4, p2tog, turn.

Cont working strap over 13 sts, slipping first st of each row and working an ssk at end of RS rows (or a p2tog at end of WS rows) while maintaining the zigzag motif. When all the shoulder sts are gone, place 13 strap sts on a holder and break yarn.

Left Shoulder

With dpn, CO 25 sts. Place 37 (44, 48, 51, 55) sts from front left shoulder and 37 (44, 48, 51, 55) sts from back left shoulder onto 2 needles. Hold back left shoulder needle in your left hand with the RS of sweater facing you and the newly CO sts in your right hand (drop front left shoulder needle for the moment. Rep from ** to complete strap.

Sleeve

Slip 23 gusset and seam sts onto shorter circular needle, join yarn at right-hand side of the gusset and seam sts and work across in pat; pick up 53 (57, 63, 71, 74) sts up the side of the armhole, work across 13 sts of the shoulder strap pat, pick up 53 (57, 63, 71, 74) sts down the other side of the armhole; pm for beg of rnd—142 (150, 162, 178, 184) sts.

Next rnd: Work seam and gusset sts as est, p53 (57, 63, 71, 74), work zigzag pat as est, p53 (57, 63, 71, 74).

Set-up Pat

Beg working Upper Gusset Chart and dec gusset as foll: Work seam st; ssk; k17; k2tog; seam st; k14 (18, 18, 20, 17); Cable 2 (Cable 2, Cable 4, Cable 6, Cable 8); Diamond and X Chart; Cable 2 (Cable 2, Cable 4, Cable 6, Cable 8); Bar Motif Chart; Cable 2 (Cable 2, Cable 4, Cable 6, Cable 8); zigzag motif as est; Cable 2 (Cable 2, Cable 4, Cable 6, Cable 8); Bar Motif Chart; Cable 2 (Cable 2, Cable 4, Cable 6, Cable 8); Diamond and X Chart; Cable 2 (Cable 2, Cable 4, Cable 6, Cable 8); k14 (18, 18, 20, 17).

See Upper Gusset Key and Upper Gusset

See Diamond X Chart

See Bar Motif Chart

Cont in est pat through Row 28 of Upper Gusset Chart.

Next rnd: K2tog (last gusset st with first seam st), work est pat to end of rnd.

Work 1 rnd even in est pat—121 (129, 141, 157, 163) sts.

Sleeve Shaping

Dec rnd: Work 2 seam sts, ssk, work to last 2 sts of rnd, k2tog.

Cont dec'ing 1 st at each side of the seam sts every 4th rnd for 30 (31, 32, 28, 32) more times, then every 3rd rnd for 0 (0, 3, 12, 9) times; AT THE SAME TIME, work in est pat until the Diamond and X Chart has been worked 4 times. Work Rows 1–9 once more, ending approx 8.25"/ 21cm from underarm.

Definition Ridge

Rnds 1, 3, 5, 7, 9: Purl, keeping seam sts in pat and cont with shaping.

Rnds 2, 4, 6, 8: Knit, keeping seam sts in pat and cont with shaping.

Plain Area

Cont in St st until shaping is complete—59 (63, 65, 73, 79) sts. Work even until piece measures 16.25 (16.25, 17.25, 18.25, 19.25)"/ 41.5 (41.5, 44, 46.5, 49)cm from pickup rnd.

Cuff

Work k2, p2 ribbing for 2.75"/7cm, dec 7 (7, 5, 5, 7) sts evenly spaced in first rnd—52 (56, 60, 68, 72) sts. BO in pat.

Neckband

Using shorter circular needle, join yarn to back right shoulder and k47 (47, 51, 59, 63) live sts from back holder, pick up 25 sts along left shoulder strap, k47 (47, 51, 59, 63) live sts from front holder, pick up 25 sts along right shoulder strap—144 (144, 152, 168, 176) sts.

Rnd 1: Purl, decreasing 24 (24, 24, 28, 28) sts evenly—120 (120, 128, 140, 148) sts.

Rnds 2–10: Work in k2, p2 ribbing.

BO loosely in pat.

FINISHING

Weave in ends. Block by washing and laying flat to dry.

11-Row Alphabet for Initials

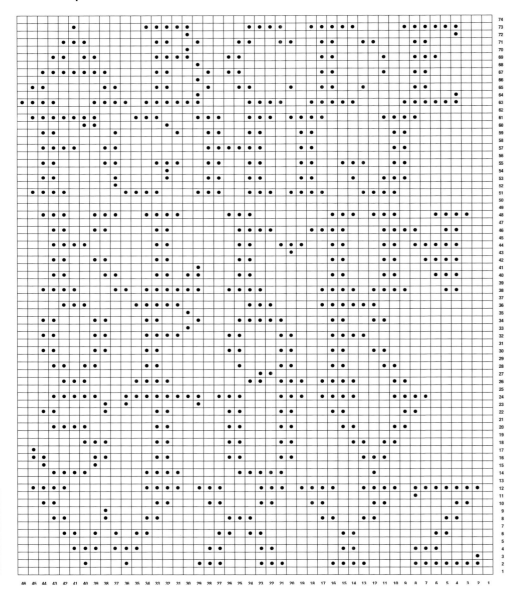

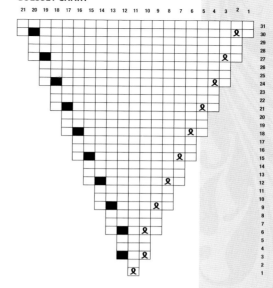

KEY 2

- ⊼ Ssk
- ⊼ K2tog
- ⊼ Centered Dbl Dec: Sl2 tog k-wise, K1, pass 2 slipped sts over
- ☐ RS: Knit
  WS: Purl
- ⊡ RS: Purl
  WS: Knit

GUSSET KEY

- ♀ Inc 1R
- ■ Inc 1L

Splitting the Work for Flat Knitting
When rnd 31 has been worked, put the gussets and seam sts (a total of 23 sts) on waste yarn.

UPPER GUESSET

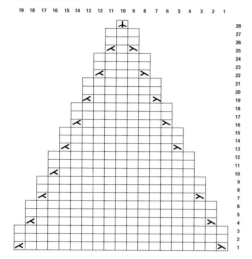

STRAP GUSSET

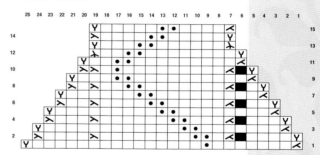

DIAMOND AND X CHART: 11 sts

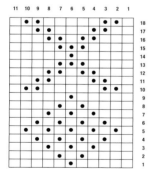

KEY

- ■ No stitch
- ⊼ RS: K2tog
  WS: P2tog
- ⊼ Ssk
- Y Slip 1 st
- ⊼ RS: Sl 1 k-wise, sl 1k-wise, k1 p2sso
  WS: P3tog
- ☐ RS: Knit
  WS: Purl
- ⊡ RS: Purl
  WS: Knit

BAR MOTIF CHART: 10 sts

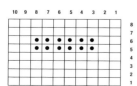

CHART A

SIZE 36: 3 sts

SIZE 40: 10 sts
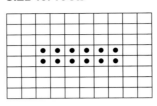

SIZE 44: 13 sts
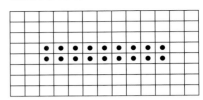

SIZE 48: 14 sts
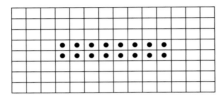

SIZE 52: 17 sts
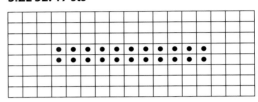

CABLE 2: 6 sts

CABLE 4: 8 sts
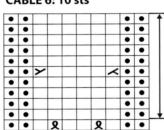

KEY 1

☐	RS Knit
●	WS Purl

CABLE 6: 10 sts

CABLE 8: 12 sts
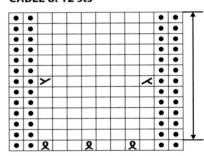

SEAM ST PATTERN

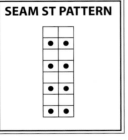

CHART E: 11 sts

CHART C: 11 sts
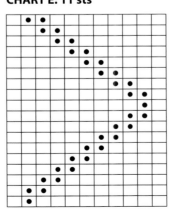
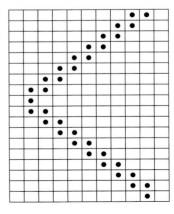

CABLE NOTATION

> ⊱⊰ C2B: K2tog but don't drop sts from left needle, knit first st again, then drop both sts from left needle.

> ⊱ ☐ ☐ ⊰ C4B: Slip 2 sts to CN and hold in back, k2, k2 from CN.

> ⊱ ☐ ☐ ☐ ☐ ⊰ C6B: Slip 3 sts to CN and hold in back, k3, k3 from CN.

> ⊱ ☐ ☐ ☐ ☐ ☐ ☐ ⊰ C8B: Slip 4 sts to CN and hold in back, k4, k4 from CN.

CHART D: 21 sts

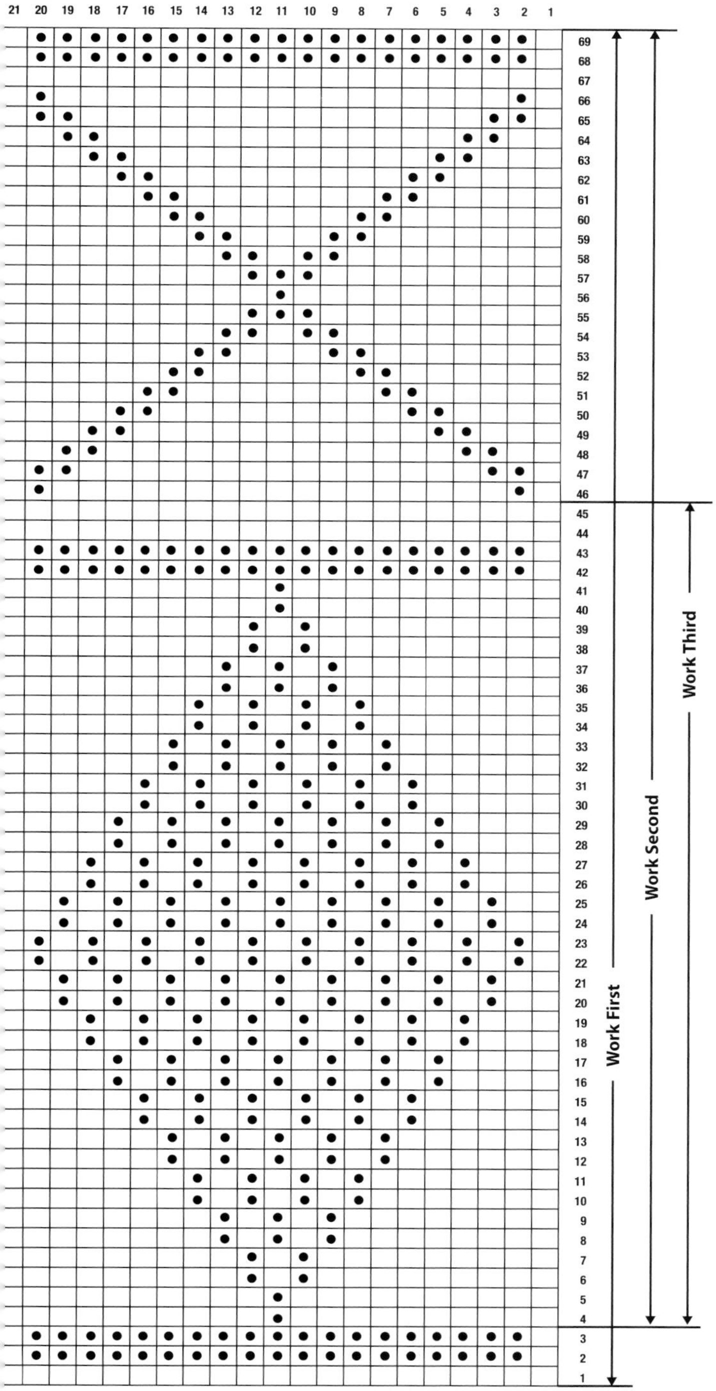

21 20 19 18 17 16 15 14 13 12 11 10 9 8 7 6 5 4 3 2 1

Rows 69–1 (numbered along right side)

Work First / Work Second / Work Third

CHART B: 21 sts

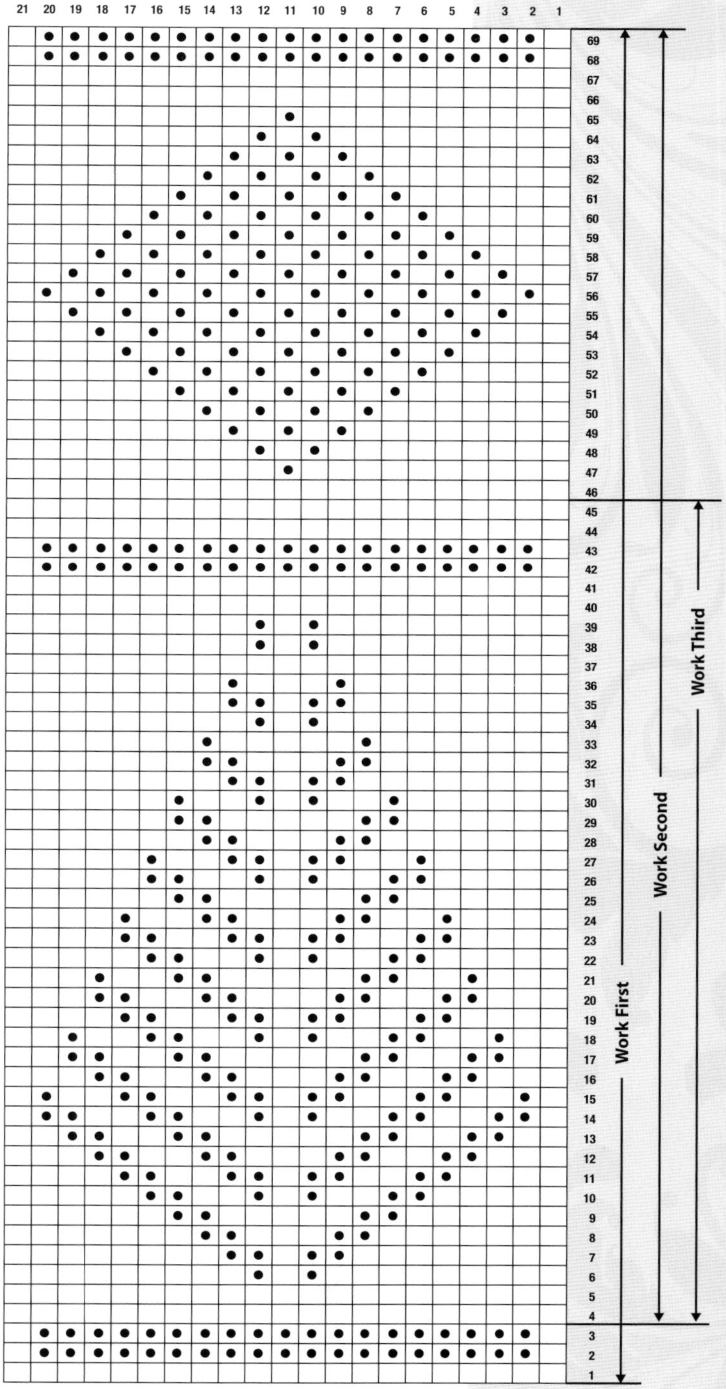

21 20 19 18 17 16 15 14 13 12 11 10 9 8 7 6 5 4 3 2 1

Rows 69–1 (numbered along right side)

Work First / Work Second / Work Third

97

SWEATERS
OF THE EAST

Turkish Delight Sweater

TURKISH DELIGHT SWEATER

DESIGN BY DONNA DRUCHUNAS

Ever since I discovered traditional, handmade Turkish socks, I have been in love with the diagonal colorwork patterns used to decorate them. In this sweater, I've expanded a traditional sock motif to cover the body and sleeves of a pullover. The pattern forms a "V" at the center front and back of the body and the sleeves are worked with the diagonals facing in opposite directions to further accentuate the mirror image around the central axis. Although Turkish lace knitting is less well known, stockings were also made with lace patterns in Anatolia and other parts of Turkey. I've used a variation of a lace ribbing pattern from a sock for the bands on this sweater, with the addition of an extra yarn over at the beginning of Round 4 to create a bias effect that complements the diagonal colorwork. ⬦

Sizes
Adult Small (**Medium**, Large)

Finished Measurements
Bust: 35 (**38**, 41)"/89 (96.5, 104)cm
Length: 22.5 (23, 23.5)"/57 (58.5, 59.5)cm

Materials 🧶 3
- Brown *Sheep Nature Spun Worsted*, 85% wool/15% mohair, 100g/3.5oz, 245yds/224g per skein: #601W Pepper (A), 4 (4, 6) skeins
- *Plymouth Boku*, 95% wool/5% silk, 50g/1.75oz, 99yds/90m per skein: #13 Rainbow (B), 7 (8, 10) skeins
- Sizes 5 (3.5mm) and 7 (4.5mm) circular needles approx 29"/73.5cm and 16"/40.5cm long and double-pointed needles or size to obtain gauge
- Tapestry needle

Gauge
20 sts and 20 rows = 4"/10cm in colorwork pattern on larger needles. *Adjust needle size as necessary to obtain correct gauge.*

PATTERN STITCHES

Ribbing

Rnds 1 and 3: (K3, p2) around.

Rnd 2: (K2tog, yo, k1, p2) around.

Rnd 4: (Yo, k1, yo, ssk, p2tog) around.

Rep Rnds 1–4 for ribbing.

Colorwork Pattern

Body (Chart A)

Right Sleeve (Chart B and B-2 Medium size)

Left Sleeve (Chart C and C-2 Medium size)

PATTERN NOTES

This sweater is knitted in-the-round from the bottom up with steek sts added for neck and armhole shaping. The sleeves are also knit in-the-round from cuff to shoulder with a reverse stockinette st facing at the armhole.

INSTRUCTIONS

Body

With smaller 29"/73.5cm long circular needle and B, CO 158 (170, 184) sts. Pm at beg of rnd and join, being careful not to twist sts. Change to A. Knit 1 row.

Work in ribbing for 3"/7.5cm.

Change to larger 29"/73.5cm long circular needle.

Next rnd: Knit and inc 16 (20, 22) sts evenly around—174 (190, 206) sts.

Place 2nd marker after 87 (95, 103) sts in for side seam.

Join 2nd color and foll chart for Body pat until piece measures 13.5" (34.5)cm from CO edge.

Armhole Steek

Next rnd: *Work to 3 sts before marker, BO 6 sts for steek opening; rep from * once.

Next rnd: Work to steek opening, CO 7 sts; rep from * once.

Cont even in Body pat and work steek sts in vertical stripes (k1A, k1B across) until piece measures 20"/51cm from CO edge.

Neck Shaping

Rnd 1: With A, work across front sts and BO center 20 (24, 24) sts for neck, weaving in B as you go (or cut B and rejoin), then work across all back sts in pat as est.

Rnd 2: Work across front to center neck bound-off sts, pm, CO 7 steek sts, pm, then work across all back sts to end of rnd.

Rnd 3: Work to 4 sts before first steek marker, with A (k2tog, k2), work steek sts in same pat as armhole steeks, sm, with A (k2, ssk), complete rnd in pat as est.

Rnd 4: Work even in est pat working sts above each dec in black.

Rep Rnds 3 and 4, 6 (8, 8) more times.

Work even in est pat until armholes measure 9 (9.5, 10)"/23 (24, 25.5)cm. BO.

Sleeves

With smaller dpns and B, CO 50 sts. Pm at beg of rnd and join, being careful not to twist sts. Change to A and work ribbing as for body for 2.5"/6.5cm.

Change to larger dpns and St st.

Next rnd: Knit, inc 9 sts evenly around—59 sts.

Foll sleeve chart (sleeve chart is shown for Medium size; adjust chart pat as necessary for Small and Large sizes), inc 1 st on each side of marker every 2nd rnd 2 (4, 6) times, then every 4th rnd 13 (14, 15) times, working incs into pat and changing to 16"/40.5cm long circular needle when sts no longer fit on dpns—89 (95, 101) sts. Work even in pat until sleeve measures 18.5 (19, 19.5)"/47 (48.5, 49.5)cm from CO edge.

Cut B. With A, work around in rev St st (purl every rnd) for .5"/1.25cm for armhole facing.

BO.

Finishing

With sewing machine, sew 2 rows of straight stitching on each side of the center st in each steek. Cut steeks open.

Sew shoulder seams. Sew sleeves into armholes. Cover cut steek with facing and tack in place.

Collar

Fold the neck steek to the inside and tack in place.

With smaller 16"/40.5cm long circular needle and A, beg at left shoulder, pick up 105 (110, 110) sts around neck opening.

Work in ribbing for 2"/5cm, ending with Rnd 1 or 3.

Dec rnd: (K3, p2tog) around.

Work even for 1"/2.5cm. BO in pat.

Weave in ends. Wash and dry flat to block.

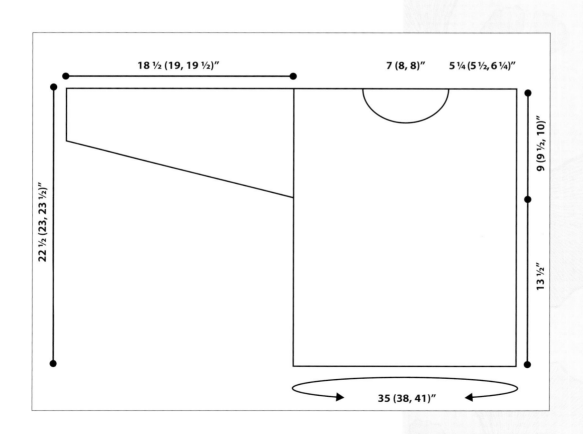

18 ½ (19, 19 ½)"

7 (8, 8)"   5 ¼ (5 ½, 6 ¼)"

9 (9 ½, 10)"

22 ½ (23, 23 ½)"

13 ½"

35 (38, 41)"

Body All Sizes (Chart A)

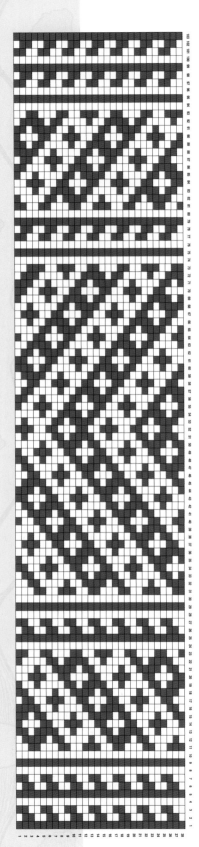

Right Sleeve All Sizes (Chart B)

Left Sleeve All Sizes (Chart C)

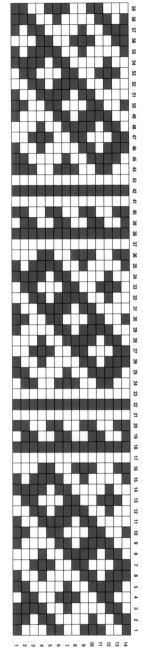

KEY	
□	**Knit** **RS:** Knit **WS:** Purl
⅄	**Left Lifted Increase** **RS:** insert needle into st below st on right needle, knit this st **WS:** insert needle into st below st on right needle, knit this st
⅄	**Right-Lifted Increase** **RS and WS:** insert needle into st below st on left needle, knit this st
▨	**No Stitch**

Left Sleeve Shaping Medium Size (Chart C-2)

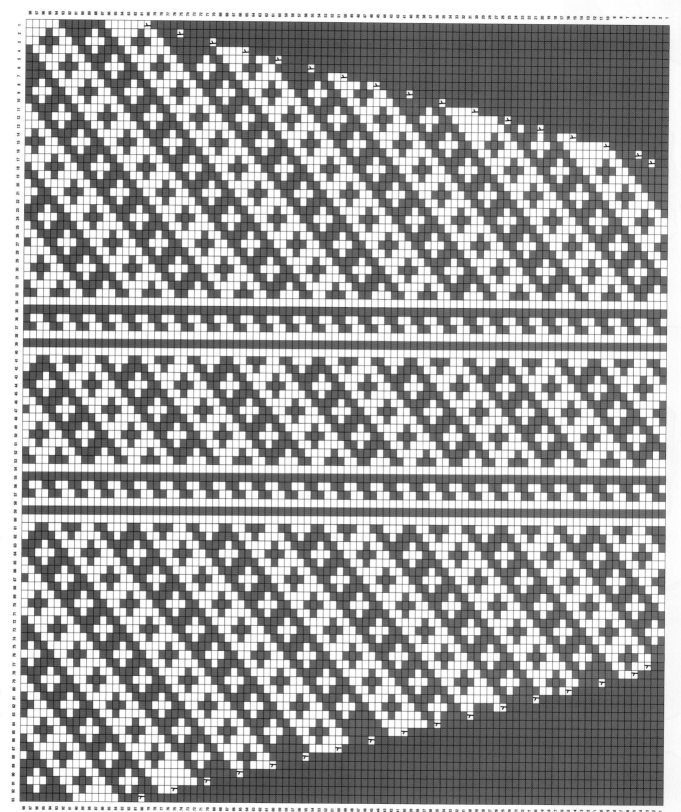

RUSSIAN PEASANT BLOUSE

DESIGN BY DONNA DRUCHUNAS

I've loved peasant blouses since the 1970s, when I discovered the beauty of folkwear sewing patterns, and I've wanted to make one ever since. I never did get around to sewing one, but this knitted design more than makes up for that. Inspired by the traditional clothing worn by Russian peasants, I worked the red and white patterning on the neck and cuffs in stranded knitting rather than embroidery. The lace pattern at the hem adds extra decorative flair. The blouse body and sleeves are both quite long, and are intended to be drawn in—at the waist with a drawstring and at the wrists with the wide cuffs—to form a graceful, flowing shape. The alpaca yarn is knit at a much looser gauge than normal to create a soft, flowing fabric, perfect for this blouse. The colorwork is knitted with smaller needles to provide more body. ❧

Sizes
Woman's **Small** (Medium, Large)

Finished Measurements
Bust: **37** (40, 43.5)"/94 (101.5, 110.5)cm
Length: 30 (31, 31)"/76 (78.5, 78.5)cm

Materials 🧶4🧶
◆ Blue Sky Alpacas *Alpaca Silk*, 50% alpaca/50% silk, 50g/1.75oz, 146yds/133m per skein: #120 White (MC), 9 (9, 10) skeins; #123 Ruby (CC), 2 skeins

◆ Size 7 (4.5mm)16"/40.5cm and 29"/73.5cm long circular and double-pointed needles or size to obtain gauge
◆ Size 5 (3.5mm) 29"/73.5 long and double-pointed needles
◆ Crochet hook size G-6 (4mm)
◆ Tapestry needle

Gauge
18 sts = 4"/10cm over St st solid and colorwork pat with larger needles
22 sts = 4"/10cm over colorwork pat with smaller needles
Adjust needle size as necessary to obtain correct gauge.

PATTERN NOTES

This sweater is worked in-the-round from the hem to the underarms; the sleeves are worked separately in-the-round from cuff to underarm. The pieces are then joined and the yoke is worked in-the-round with an optional steeked front opening.

STITCH PATTERN

Lace Border (multiple of 14 sts)

Rnd 1: *K4tog, yo, [k1, yo] 5 times, k4togtbl, p1; rep from * around.

Rnd 2: *K13, p1; rep from * around.

Rep Rnds 1–2 for Lace Border.

INSTRUCTIONS

Body

With larger 29"/73.5cm long circular needle and MC, CO 168 (182, 196) sts. Place first marker at beg of rnd and 2nd marker after 84 (91, 98) sts for side seam, then join being careful not to twist sts.

Work around in Lace Border pat for 6"/15cm.

Change to St st and work even for 3"/7.5cm.

Eyelet rnd: (Yo, k2tog) around.

Cont to work even in St st until piece measures 13 (14, 15)"/33 (35.5, 38) cm from CO edge.

Short Rows

Note: If desired, work 4 sets of short rows so back of sweater does not ride up. To work a short row set, start at a side marker and:

Row 1 (RS): K3 sts before 2nd marker. Wrap and turn (w&t).

Row 2 (WS): P3 sts before first marker, w&t.

Rep Rows 1 and 2 three more times, working 2 or 3 fewer sts before the w&t each time.

Return to knitting in-the-round, remembering to hide the wrapped sts when you work them and mark this as the back.

Work until back measures 18 (19, 19)"/45.5 (48.5, 48.5)cm from CO edge.

On next rnd, place 9 (9, 10) sts on hold at each side seam, with half of underarm sts before side seam marker and half after—75 (82, 88) sts rem for front and for back. Remove markers.

Set body aside, placing sts on a spare needle or holders.

Sleeves

Using smaller dpns and MC, CO 48 sts. Pm at beg of rnd and join, taking care not to twist sts. Foll Cuff Chart (12-st rep) colorwork pat until all rows of chart have been worked.

Cut CC, change to larger dpns.

Work in St st, inc as foll on first rnd: (k4, m1) around—60 sts.

Cont in St st, inc 1 st at beg and end of rnd every 4th rnd 10 (10, 12) times—80 (80, 84) sts.

Work even until sleeve measures 20"/51cm from CO edge changing to the 16"/40.5cm long circular needles when the sts no longer fit comfortably on dpns.

On next rnd, place 9 (9, 10) sts on hold at each side seam for underarms, with half of the sts before the side seam marker and other half after—71 (71, 74) sts.

Remove markers. Set sleeve aside, putting sts on a spare needle or holder.

Rep for 2nd sleeve.

Yoke

Slip body and sleeve sts on larger 29"/73.5 long circular needle as foll: 75 (82, 88) back yoke sts, pm, 71 (71, 74) sleeve sts, pm, 75 (82, 88) front yoke sts, pm, 71 (71, 74) sleeve sts, place a CC marker for beg of rnd—292 (306, 324) sts.

Work even in St st for 1"/2.5cm.

Neck Opening

Next rnd: Knit and at center front, BO 2 sts for neck opening—290 (304, 322) sts.

Next rnd: Knit and CO 7 sts for steek over BO sts (do not count steek sts).

Work until yoke measures 4.5"/11.5cm.

Next rnd: (K2, k2tog) around to last 2 (0, 2) sts, k2 (0, 2)—218 (228, 242) sts.

Work until yoke measures 6"/15cm.

Next rnd: (K1, k2tog) around to last 2 (0, 2) sts, k2 (0, 2)—146 (152, 162) sts.

Work until yoke measures 9"/23cm.

Next rnd: Knit and dec 22 (28, 38) sts evenly around—124 sts.

Collar

Change to smaller 16"/40.5cm circular needle and work Neckband Chart (12-st rep) colorwork pat across center 120 sts with 2 extra sts at each end; AT THE SAME TIME, working steek sts for neck opening in vertical stripes (k1 MC, k1 CC).

Change to larger 29"/73.5cm long circular needle and work eyelet rnd as for waist.

Knit 2 rnds.

Work in Lace Border pat for 1"/2.5cm. BO loosely in pat.

Finishing

Using 3-needle bind-off or Kitchener stitch, join underarm seams.

Weave in ends. Wash and dry flat to block.

Neck Opening (optional)

With sewing machine, sew 2 rows of straight stitching on each side of the center st in each steek. Cut neck opening, fold back facings and tack in place.

Option 1: Simple opening—work 1 row of single crochet along both sides of steeked opening, working sc2tog (dec) in each corner. Fasten off.

Option 2: Lacing eyelets—work 1 row of single crochet as for simple opening as foll:

Ch1, turn, *6 sc, ch 3, skip 3 sc; rep from * to bottom working sc2tog (dec) in corners, then work sc up 2nd side of opening placing ch-3 spaces aligned with those on first side. Fasten off.

Twisted Cord Ties

With CC, make 2 twisted cords desired length and attach at waist and neck opening as a drawstring through the eyelets or as lacing through the crochet openings.

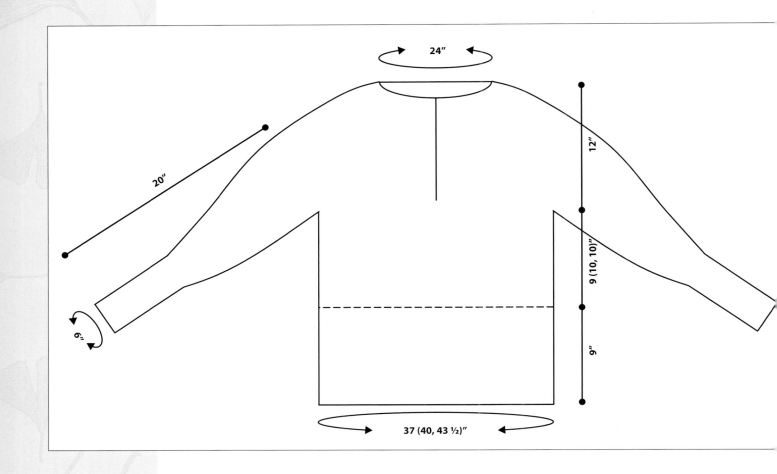

Neckband Chart

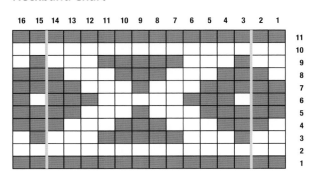

	KEY	
	KEY	
☐	#120 White (MC)	
■	#123 Ruby (CC)	

Cuff Chart

JAPANESE KIMONO

DESIGN BY PINPILAN WANGSAI

The traditional men's kimono is a very simple yet versatile outfit. It is warm enough to wear in cool weather, you can tuck your hands inside the sleeves if it gets chilly, and when it gets a bit warmer, the opening under the armholes lets in enough air so your body can breathe. But my favorite part is that you can store small stuff inside the sleeves. In modern-day Tokyo, a lot of people have given up wearing the kimono for more trendy modern clothes, but I still think kimonos have a certain old-world charm. So with the versatile ideals of the original in mind, I made up this pattern as a shorter, more casual take on the old style so you can wear it everyday over your regular clothing. The name *kumo* means clouds and comes from the white intarsia cloud details on the front and back. The Merino wool makes this sweater soft enough to wear next to your skin on warm spring days, and the opening under the arm allows it to fit easily over any other shirt for colder climates. The firmer cotton sash holds the whole thing in place. ❧

Sizes
Small (**Medium**, Large, XLarge, XXLarge)

Finished Measurements
Chest: 33 (36, 39, 42, 45)"/84 (91.5, 99, 106.5, 114.5)cm
Length: 26 (28, 30, 32, 34)"/66 (71, 76, 81.5, 86.5)cm

Materials 🧶4
- Munsell Merino 150 Rainbow, 100% Merino wool, 40g/1.5oz; 99yds/88m per skein: #96 Navy (MC), 19 (21, 23, 25, 27) skeins
- Rowan Handknit Cotton, 100% cotton, 50g/1.75oz, 94yds/85m per skein: Ecru (CC), 1 (1, 1, 1, 1) skein

- ◆ Size 7 (4.5mm) straight needles or size to obtain gauge
- ◆ Size 7 (4.5mm) double-point needle or one 36"/91.5cm long circular needle
- ◆ Stitch markers
- ◆ 4 stitch holders
- ◆ Tapestry needle

Gauge
20 sts and 28 rows = 4"/10cm in St st on larger needles
Adjust needle size as necessary to obtain correct gauge.

PATTERN NOTES

If you can't find Munsell's yarn outside of Japan, Merino Fine *Pure Merino Yarn* (100% Pure New Zealand Washable Super Fine Merino, 50g/1.75oz, 110yds/100m) is a good substitute. Color #220 is closest to the main color used.

The neck edges on the front of the sweater are decreased on both the knit and purl side to achieve an even, steep slant. The following stitch is used to make a left-slanting decrease on the wrong side. It's used only for the right front piece.

p2tb: purl 2 together through back loop

INSTRUCTIONS

Back

With straight needles and MC, CO 82 (90, 98, 106, 112) sts. Work in k1, p1 ribbing for 1.5"/4cm. Change to St st and work until piece measures 19 (21, 23, 25, 27)"/48.5 (53.5, 58.5, 63.5, 68.5)cm from CO edge, ending after a WS row.

Row 1 (RS): K29 (33, 37, 41, 44), foll intarsia pat for Cloud Motif 1 across 25 sts, knit to end.

Rows 2–36: Cont to foll chart.

Work even in St st for 2"/5cm.

Transfer 28 (30, 33, 35, 38) sts to holder.

Next row: BO 26 (30, 32, 36, 36) sts, then transfer rem 28 (30, 33, 35, 38) sts to a holder.

Right Front

With straight needles and MC, CO 79 (84, 91, 96, 103) sts.

Work in k1, p1 ribbing for 1.5"/4cm, ending after a WS row.

Next row: P5, knit to end.

Next row: Purl to end.

Rep last 2 rows until piece measures 5 (5.5, 6, 6.5, 7)"/12.5 (14, 15, 16.5, 18)cm, ending after a WS row. Pm on last st.

Shaping

Next row: K2, k2tog, knit to end.

Next row: Purl.

Next row: Knit.

Next row: Purl to last 4 sts, p2togb, p2.

Next row: Knit.

Next row: Purl.

Cont as est working 1 dec as above every 3rd row; AT THE SAME TIME, when piece measures 20 (22, 24, 26, 28)"/51 (56, 61, 66, 71)cm and there are 44 (46, 49, 51, 54) sts on needle, beg Cloud Motif 2 as foll:

RS: K21 (23, 23, 25, 25), work Cloud Motif 2 across next 11 sts, knit to end.

Work intarsia pat for 8 rows, cont decs until 28 (30, 33, 35, 38) sts rem. Transfer sts to holder.

Left Front

With straight needles and MC, CO 79 (84, 91, 96, 103) sts.

Work in k1, p1 ribbing for 1.5"/4cm, ending after a WS row.

Next row: Knit to last 4 sts, purl to end.

Next row: Purl.

Rep last 2 rows until piece measures 5 (5.5, 6, 6.5, 7)"/12.5 (14, 15, 16.5, 18) cm, ending after a WS row. Pm on last st.

Shaping

Next row: Knit to last 4 sts, k2tog. k2.

Next row: Purl.

Next row: Knit.

Next row: P2, p2tog, purl to end.

Next row: Knit.

Next row: Purl.

Cont as est working 1 dec as above every 3rd row; AT THE SAME TIME, when piece measures 20 (22, 24, 26, 28)"/51 (56, 61, 66, 71)cm and there are 44 (46, 49, 51, 54) sts on needle, beg Cloud Motif 3 as foll:

RS: K12 (12, 15, 15, 18), work Cloud Motif 3 across next 11 sts, knit to end.

Work intarsia pat for 8 rows, cont decs until 28 (30, 33, 35, 38) sts rem. Transfer sts to holder.

Sleeves

With straight needles and MC, CO 70 (75, 80, 85, 90) sts.

Work in St st until piece measures 7 (8, 9, 10, 11)"/18 (20.5, 23, 25.5, 28)cm from CO edge, ending after a WS row.

Next row: P5, knit to end.

Next row: Purl.

Rep last 2 rows until piece measures 23 (24, 25, 26, 27)"/58.5 (61, 63.5, 66, 68.5)cm from CO edge, ending after a WS row.

Change to St st and work until piece measures 30 (32, 34, 36, 38)"/76 (81.5, 86.5, 91.5, 96.5)cm from CO edge. BO.

Fold sleeve in half crosswise and pm on the fold on the shoulder edge (the side with no border st).

Sash

With straight needles and using CC, CO 10 sts. Work in garter st until sash is long enough to tie around your waist once. BO.

Finishing

Join back to front at shoulders using Kitchener stitch. Pm on sleeve edge of seams.

Collar Band

Beg at marker on left front, using dpns or circular needle, pick up 125 (135, 140, 155, 165) sts evenly up along left front neck edge, 28 (30, 32, 36, 36) sts along back neck and 125 (135, 140, 155, 165) sts evenly down along right front neck edge until you reach marker. If using dpns, divide sts evenly between 3 dpns. Do not join. Work back and forth in garter st until band is 2"/5cm wide. BO.

Match marker on shoulder seam of body to marker on fold of sleeves. Join sleeve to body 10 (11, 12, 13, 14)"/25.5 (28, 30.5, 33, 35.5)cm before marker and 10 (11, 12, 13, 14)"/25.5 (28, 30.5, 33, 35.5)cm after marker.

Beg on sleeve cuff edge where border stops, sew down to bottom of sleeves, sew across bottom of sleeves and 2"/5cm up toward armhole seam, leaving a 3"/7.5cm opening from here to where the armhole seam starts. Join body seam from waist up until 3"/7.5cm to where armhole seam starts.

Weave in all ends.

Note: When wearing kimono, be sure the left front goes over the right. The collar band should form a "Y" shape. Tie the sash just above your hip.

Cloud Motif 1 Chart

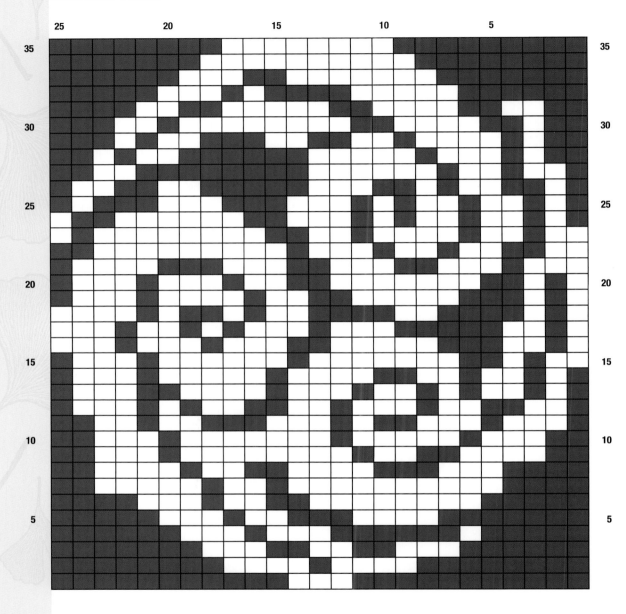

KEY

☐ MC1

■ MC2

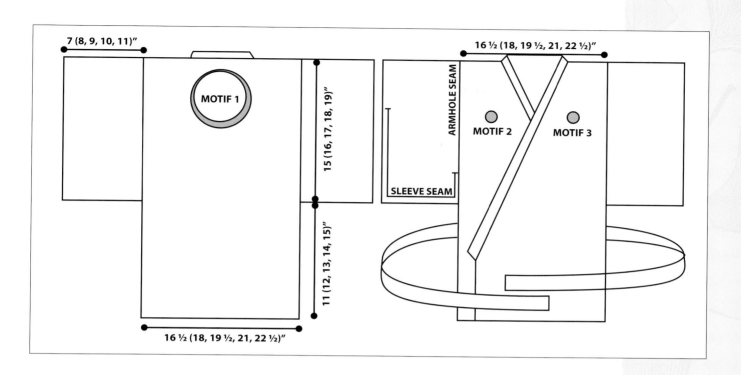

7 (8, 9, 10, 11)"

MOTIF 1

15 (16, 17, 18, 19)"

11 (12, 13, 14, 15)"

16 ½ (18, 19 ½, 21, 22 ½)"

16 ½ (18, 19 ½, 21, 22 ½)"

ARMHOLE SEAM

SLEEVE SEAM

MOTIF 2

MOTIF 3

Cloud Motif 2 Chart

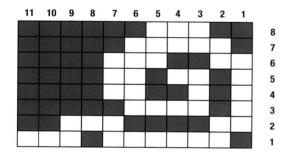

11 10 9 8 7 6 5 4 3 2 1

8
7
6
5
4
3
2
1

Cloud Motif 3 Chart

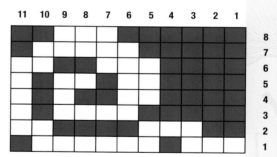

11 10 9 8 7 6 5 4 3 2 1

8
7
6
5
4
3
2
1

117

SWEATERS
OF THE WEST

COWICHAN-INSPIRED SWALLOWS & IVY WRAP CARDIGAN

DESIGN BY DAWN BROCCO

Swallows & Ivy is a wrap cardigan in the Cowichan style, but with modern twists. Though the Cascade Pastaza yarn resembles a handspun singles yarn, as the Cowichans spun and used in their knitting, it is made of llama and wool, making the cardigan soft and luxurious, therefore appealing to modern, feminine tastes. The main swallow motif floats on a stockinette stitch background. Only the ivy motif borders the lower edge of the cardigan and the sleeves. This sweater is slightly oversized for a cozy, blanket look. ∙∾

Sizes
Adult Small (**Medium**, Large)

Finished Measurements
Chest: 46 (51, 56)"/117 (129.5,142)cm
Length: 26 (27, 28)"/66 (68.5, 71)cm

Materials (4)
- Cascade Yarns *Pastaza*, 50% Llama/50% wool; 100g/3.5oz; 132yds/121m per skein:
- Ecru #002 (MC), 15 (17, 19) skeins; Walnut Heather #027 (A) and Chocolate #063 (B), 2 skeins each

- Size 11 (8mm) 16"/40.5cm and 32"/81.5–40"/101.5cm circular and double-pointed needles or size needed to obtain gauge
- Two size 10 (6mm) double-pointed needles
- Stitch pins
- Waste yarn or stitch holder
- Tapestry needle

Gauge
12 sts and 16 rows = 4"/10cm in St st on larger needles with doubled yarn
Adjust needle size as necessary to obtain correct gauge.

PATTERN NOTES

Yarn is held double throughout.

The body of the sweater is knit back and forth in one piece until the bottom of the armholes, then it is worked back and forth on the front and the back of the sweater.

The sleeves are knit circularly from the top down.

Cowichan shoulder bind-off is used at the shoulders to create a decorative seam and provides 2 of the sleeve sts, at the top of sleeve.

The afterthought pockets are optional and are worked last.

INSTRUCTIONS

Body

With MC and longer size 11 (8mm) circular needle, using long-tail cast-on, CO 122 (138, 154) sts. *Do not join.*

Row 1 (WS): (P2, k2) across, end p2.

Row 2 (RS): (K2, p2) across, end k2.

Rep last 2 rows for k2, p2 rib 7 times more (approx 4.25"/11cm from CO edge, unstretched).

Purl next WS row.

Work 1 rep (12 rows) Ivy Body Chart breaking off B after Row 6 and breaking off A after Row 12.

Work 35 rows St st with MC or until piece measures 17"/43cm from the CO edge, ending after a RS row.

Divide for Armholes

Next row (WS): P27 (31, 35) left front sts, turn—68 (76, 84) back sts and 27 (31, 35) right front sts rem unworked. Place these rem sts on waste yarn or holder.

Left Front

Note: Swallow Chart is worked centered vertically on front; V-neck shaping occurs at same time. Read through instructions before working.

V-Neck Decs and Left Swallow Chart

Work 6 (10, 14) more rows St st, ending after a WS row.

Dec row (RS): Work in pat to last 3 sts, k2tog, k1.

Work in pat 7 (5, 3) rows even.

Rep Dec row.

Rep last 8 (6, 4) rows 2 (3, 4) times more.

Work 1 (1, 5) row(s) even—23 (26, 29) shoulder sts rem.

AT THE SAME TIME, beg Left Swallow Chart on RS Row 8 (10, 12), then work 8 (10, 12) rows of St st after finishing 17 rows of chart.

Break yarn. Place rem 23 (26, 29) left shoulder sts on waste yarn or holder.

Back

Join MC to WS and work in St st on 68 (76, 84) back sts, leaving rem 23 (26, 29) right front sts on holder. Cont in St st on back sts for 36 (40, 44) rows or until armhole is 9 (10, 11)"/23 (25, 28)cm.

Note: Due to the difference in gauges between St st and stranded pat, back should have 3 more rows. Break MC. Turn work.

Place first and last 23 (26, 29) back shoulder sts on separate holders. Place 22 (24, 26) center back neck sts on another holder.

Right Front

Join MC to WS and work 27 (31, 35) right front sts from holder. Work 7 (11, 15) rows St st in all, ending after a WS row.

V-Neck Decs and Right Swallow Chart

Dec Row (RS): K1, ssk, work in pat across.

Work in pat 7 (5, 3) rows even.

Rep Dec row.

Rep last 8 (6, 4) rows 2 (3, 4) times more.

Work 1 (1, 5) row(s) even—23 (26, 29) shoulder sts rem.

AT THE SAME TIME, beg Right Swallow Chart on RS Row 8 (10, 12), then work 8 (10, 12) rows of St st after finishing 17 rows of chart.

Break yarn. Leave sts on needle.

Cowichan Shoulder Bind-Off

Note: BO works from the neck edge to the sleeve edge.

Right Front to Back

Place 23 (26, 29) right back shoulder sts on separate needle. Hold right front shoulder sts parallel to right back shoulder sts, with WS's of fabric facing each other (RS of front facing you). Beg at neck edge, with smaller dpn and MC, knit 1 st on front needle.

Twist dpn counterclockwise and purl 1 st on rear needle.

Twist dpn clockwise and knit 2nd st on front needle, pass first knit st over 2nd knit st.

Twist dpn counterclockwise and purl 2nd st on rear needle, pass first purl st over 2nd purl st.

Cont to knit 1 st on front needle and BO, then twist dpn to purl 1 st on rear needle and BO, until 1 st rem on each needle. Place these 2 rem sts on holder.

Left Front to Back

Place 23 (26, 29) left back shoulder and left front shoulder sts on separate needles. BO as for right front to back, but with back shoulder sts facing you as you work from neck edge to sleeve edge. Place 2 rem sts on holder.

Sleeves

With MC and shorter size 11 (8mm) circular needle, beg at center underarm, pick up and knit 26 (29, 32) sts along selvedge edge of armhole opening to shoulder, knit 2 shoulder sts from holder, then pick up and knit 26 (29, 32) sts along selvedge edge of armhole opening to underarm, pm.

Note: If you need to pick up an extra st along the back edge, then dec it on next rnd.

Shaping

Note: For smoother dec st symmetry at underarm, work the end of rnd dec at the end of the previous rnd, before working the dec at the beg of next rnd.

Size Small/Medium: Knit 2 rnds.

Dec rnd: K1, k2tog, knit to within 2 sts from end, ssk.

Knit 3 rnds.

Rep Dec rnd.

Rep last 7 rnds 4 times more. Knit 2 rnds. Rep Dec rnd—32 sts rem.

Size Medium/Large: Knit 2 rnds.

Dec rnd: K1, k2tog, knit to within 2 sts from end, ssk.

Knit 1 rnd.

Rep Dec rnd.

Rep last 5 rnds 6 times more. Knit 1 rnd—32 sts rem.

Size Large/XLarge: Knit 1 rnd.

Dec Rnd: K1, k2tog, knit to within 2 sts from end, ssk.

Rep last 2 rnds 16 times more—32 sts rem.

Note: Sleeve should measure 9.75 (9.25, 8.75)"/25 (23.5, 22)cm or work until 8.25"/21cm less than desired length.

Work Ivy Sleeve Chart 16-st rep until complete, without any further shaping.

On next rnd, dec 8 (4, 4) sts evenly around—24 (28, 28) sts rem.

Work 17 rnds of k2, p2 rib.

BO in rib. Break yarn.

Front Bands

With MC, longer size 11 (8mm) needle and RS facing, beg at lower right front edge, pick up and knit 55 sts along between lower edge and first neck shaping row.

Row 1 (WS): P3, (k2, p2) across.

Row 2 (RS): (K2, p2) across, end k3.

Rows 3–10 (12, 14): Rep last 2 rows 4 (5, 6) times more.

Turning ridge: On next WS row, knit across.

On next RS row, resume rib and work for 9 (11, 13) rows.

BO in rib.

Work front band along left front edge in the same way, picking up and knitting sts from first neck shaping row to lower edge.

With one strand yarn and tapestry needle, tack inside of front bands to the pickup "seam," making sure bands lie flat.

Shawl Collar

Working in Yarn Ends

1. RS and WS is given, as collar is being worked; however, once the collar is finished, the WS will be facing you, after the collar is folded down.

2. First sts are not slipped, unless otherwise noted, but can be worked snugly to alleviate gaps.

Right Front Collar

(RS): With MC and longer size 11 (8mm) needle, beg at first knit st on front band past the turning ridge, pick up and knit 10 (11, 14) sts along top edge of front band, making sure to go knit up through both layers of fabric, then pick up and knit 2 sts along neck shaping edge, turn.

Setup Rib:

Sizes Small/Medium and Large/XLarge (WS): (P2, k2) across, turn.

Size Medium/Large (WS): K1, (p2, k2) across, turn.

All sizes: Work k2, p2 rib across, pick up and knit 2 more sts along neck shaping edge, turn.

Sizes Small/Medium and Large/XLarge: (K2, p2) across, end k2, turn.

Size Medium/Large: P1, (k2, p2) across, end k2, turn.

All sizes: Cont to work back and forth in k2, p2 rib, picking up and knitting 2 sts along neck edge, at end of every RS row to the shoulder. Cont rib pat into 2 shoulder "seam" sts. Place sts on holder.

Left Front Collar

(RS): With MC and longer size 11 (8mm) needle, pick up and knit 2 sts along neck shaping edge, then 10 (11, 14) sts along top edge of front band, making sure to knit up through both layers of fabric, with last knit-up st in last knit st of band, turn.

Setup Rib:

Sizes Small/Medium and Large/XLarge (WS): (K2, p2) across, bring yarn forward, pick up and purl 2 more sts along neck shaping edge, turn.

Size Medium/Large (WS): (K2, p2) across, end k1, bring yarn forward, pick up and purl 2 more sts along neck shaping edge, turn.

Sizes Small/Medium and Large/XLarge: (P2, k2) across, end p2, turn.

Size Medium/Large: K1, (p2, k2) across, end p2, turn.

All sizes: Cont to work back and forth in rib, picking up and purling 2 sts along neck edge, at end of every WS row to the shoulder. Cont rib pat into 2 shoulder "seam" sts.

Sizes Small/Medium and Large/XLarge end with p2 at the shoulder. Size Medium/Large ends with a k1 at the shoulder.

Back Collar

Setup Rib and Join: Place 22 (24, 26) back neck sts on the longer size 11 (8mm) needle. Place the held Right Front Collar sts on shorter needle, temporarily.

Sizes Small/Medium and Large/XLarge (RS): With MC and RS facing, slip first st, k1, (p2, k2) 5 (6) times, p1 (first of shoulder seam sts), p3tog last shoulder st with 2 adjoining left front collar sts, place pin in dec st, turn.

Size Medium/Large (RS): With MC and RS facing, slip first st, (p2, k2) 6 times, p1, p3tog next purl st with 2 adjoining left front collar sts, place pin in dec st, turn.

All sizes (WS): Slip first st, rib across WS row to pinned st, sssk, turn.

Slipping first st on each row, work back and forth, dec 2 sts at end of each row 3 times more, ending after a WS row. **Note:** Rib pat should now flow evenly across entire collar—82 (86, 94) sts rem.

On next RS row, pat to pinned st, pat 4 more sts, turn.

Sl 1, pat to pinned st, pat 4 more sts, turn.

Rep last 2 rows until all front sts have been worked, ending after a WS row.

BO loosely.

Afterthought Pockets

With waste yarn, run a thread along the ditch between st #'s 4 and 5 (6 and 7, 8 and 9) from the front band. Count 18 sts from this marker and run a thread along the next ditch. Count 9 MC St st rows from the last Ivy Body Chart row and run a thread through this row between the 2 markers.

Snip the center st between the 2 vertical thread markers in Row 10 (the row above the thread marker). Unravel the sts in either direction, freeing up upper and lower sts and a length of yarn on each side.

Place the upper sts on a holder, include 1/2 st on each side—19 sts.

Pocket Trim

Place lower 18 sts onto size 10 (6mm) dps and with RS facing, join yarn and knit across, turn. Knit 5 more rows. BO. Break yarn.

Pocket Lining

Place upper sts on size 10 (6mm) dpn and work 29 rows St st—6"/15cm. BO.

Tie

With A and larger size 11 (8mm) needle, long-tail cast-on 180 (194, 208) sts, turn. Knit across.

*With B, knit 2 rows. With A, knit 2 rows. Rep from * once more. BO with A.

Finishing

Tack pocket linings along WS. Tack sides of pocket trim along RS.

Weave in all yarn ends to WS.

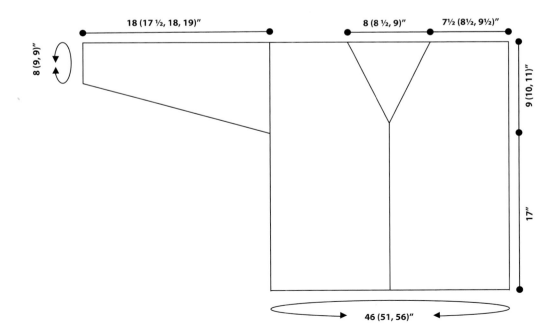

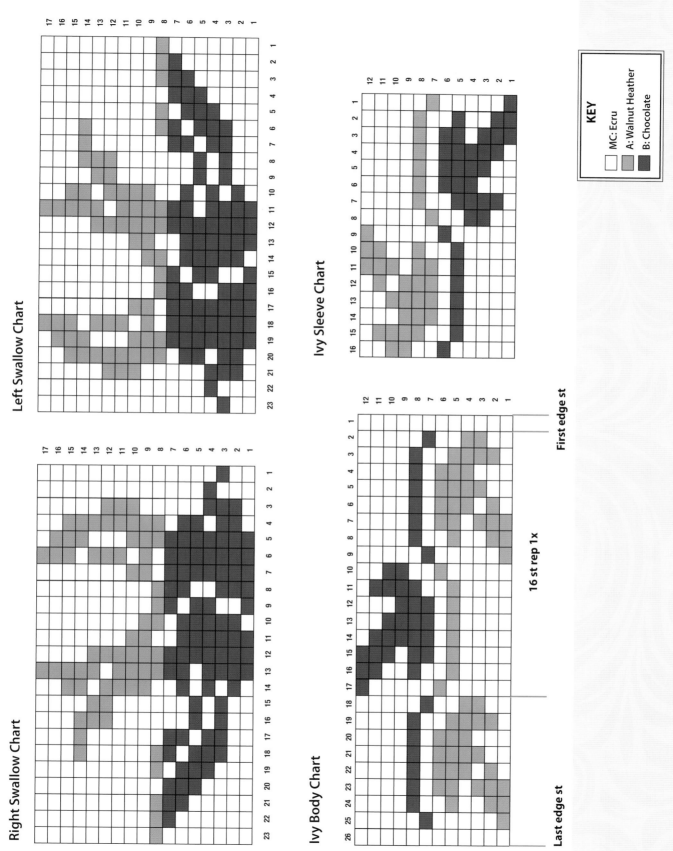

Left Swallow Chart

Right Swallow Chart

Ivy Sleeve Chart

Ivy Body Chart

16 st rep 1x

First edge st

Last edge st

KEY

☐ MC: Ecru
▨ A: Walnut Heather
■ B: Chocolate

127

ANDEAN CONDOR HOODIE WITH HANDWARMERS

DESIGN BY CYNTHIA LECOUNT SAMAKÉ

This cozy, oversized hoodie has built-in handwarmers, great for driving, knitting, and dog walking in a chilly climate. And if the weather gets warmer, just turn the ribbing back to make cuffs. The Andean condor motif on the pocket shows up on many woven and knitted textiles throughout the Andes. The ultra-soft yarn is the cushiest 100 percent wool that I've ever used. ❧

Sizes
Adult **Small** (Medium, Large)

Finished Measurements
Chest: **44** (48, 52.5)"/112 (122, 133.5)cm
Length: 25 (26, 27/5)"/63.5 (66, 70)cm

Materials 🧶 4
- GGH *Magica*, distributed by Muench, 100% wool, 1.75oz/50g, 99yds/90m per ball: Teal #3 (A), 13 (15, 17) balls

- Lana Grossa *Joker*, 80% wool/20% nylon, 1.75oz/50g, 88yds/80m per ball: Black #12 (B), 1 ball
- Sizes 6 (4mm) and 7 (4.5mm) needles or size needed to obtain gauge
- Split ring stitch markers
- Tapestry needle

Gauge
16 sts and 24 rows = 4"/10cm in St st on larger needles
Adjust needle size as necessary to obtain correct gauge.

INSTRUCTIONS

Back

With smaller needles and A, CO 87 (95, 105) sts.

Row 1 (RS): *K1, p1; rep from * to last st, k1.

Row 2 (WS): *P1, k1; rep from * to last st, p1.

Rep these 2 rows until ribbing measures 3"/7.5cm from CO edge, ending with a WS row.

Change to larger needles and St st, inc 1 (1, 0) st on first row—88 (96, 105) sts. Work even until back measures 16 (16, 17)"/40.5 (40.5, 43)cm from CO edge, ending with a WS row.

Armhole Shaping

Row 1 (RS): BO 6 (7, 8) sts, knit to end of row—82 (89, 97) sts.

Row 2 (WS): BO 6 (7, 8) sts, purl to end of row—76 (82, 89) sts.

Cont in St st, dec 1 st each side every other row 6 (6, 7) times—64 (70, 75) sts. Work even until armholes measure 8 (9, 9.5)"/(20.5 (23, 24)cm, ending with a WS row.

Shoulder Shaping

Row 1 (RS): BO 6 (6, 7) sts, knit to end of row—58 (64, 67) sts.

Row 2 (WS): BO 6 (6, 7) sts, purl to end of row—52 (58, 61) sts.

BO 6 (7, 7) sts beg of next 4 rows—28 (30, 33) sts.

BO rem 28 (30, 33) sts for back neck.

Front

Work same as back including armhole shaping until front measures 18.5 (19, 20)"/47 (48.5, 51)cm from CO edge, ending with a WS row—64 (70, 75) sts.

Neck Opening

Sizes Small (Medium) Only

Row 1 (RS): K32 (35), drop yarn and join new ball, k32 (35).

Row 2 (WS): P32 (35), drop yarn, pick up next yarn, p32 (35) to end of row—32 (35) sts each side of neck opening.

Size Large Only

Row 1 (RS): K37, BO center st, knit to end—37 sts each side of neck opening.

All Sizes

Cont in St st working both sides of neck opening at the same time until front measures 23 (24, 25.25)"/ 58.5 (61, 64)cm from CO edge, ending with a RS row.

Row 1 (WS): P32 (35, 37), drop yarn, pick up next yarn and BO 12 (13, 13) sts at beg of neck edge, purl to end.

Row 2 (RS): K20 (22, 24) sts, pick up next yarn and BO 12 (13, 13) sts at beg of neck edge, knit to end—20 (22, 24) sts each side of neck.

Cont working both sides of neck at the same time, dec 1 st at each neck edge every other row 2 (2, 3) times—18 (20, 21) sts each side.

Work even in St st until front measures 24 (25, 26 1/2)"/61 (63.5, 67.5)cm from CO edge, ending with a WS row.

Shoulder Shaping

Row 1 (RS): BO 6 (6, 7) sts at beg of row for shoulder, knit to neck edge, drop yarn, pick up next yarn, k18 (20, 21) sts.

Row 2 (WS): BO 6 (6, 7) sts at beg of row for shoulder, purl to neck edge, pick up next yarn, purl to end of row—12 (14, 14) sts rem on each shoulder.

Row 3 (RS): BO 6 (7, 7) sts at beg of row for shoulder, knit to end.

Row 4 (WS): BO 6 (7, 7) sts at beg of row for shoulder, purl to end.

BO rem 6 (7, 7) sts on each shoulder. Cut yarns leaving 4"/10cm tails.

Right Sleeve

Note: Both sleeves are made the same, with thumb holes worked into the long ribbed cuff section. The thumb holes must be made on opposite sides of the ribbing before beginning the St st. You will be working the cuff upward toward the upper sleeve, but the hand enters the cuff downward from the upper sleeve.

With smaller needles and A, CO 31 (35, 41) sts.

Cuff: Work in k1, p1 ribbing same as body for 2.5"/6.5cm.

Thumb hole opening: Rib 8 sts as est, drop yarn, join 2nd ball of yarn and BO 2 sts, work in est rib to end of row—29 (33, 39) sts.

Working both sides of the thumb opening at the same time, with separate balls of yarn, cont in est rib until thumb opening measures about 1.5"/4cm from BO. Close thumbhole opening.

Next row: Work in est rib across to thumb hole opening, CO 2 sts over BO sts using the backward loop method, drop 2nd ball of yarn and cont in est rib to end of row.

Work even in ribbing for another 3"/7.5cm measured from thumb hole closing.

Note: Total rib length should be about 7"/18cm from CO edge. Cut 2nd ball of yarn at thumb hole leaving 4"/10cm tail.

Sleeve Shaping

Change to larger needles and St st beg with a RS row and inc 1 st—32 (36, 42) sts.

Cont in St st inc 1 st each side every 4th row 6 (10, 6) times, then every 6th row 10 (8, 11) times—64 (72, 76) sts. Work even until sleeve measures 22 (22.5, 23)"/56 (57, 58.5)cm from CO edge, ending with a WS row.

Cap Shaping

Row 1 (RS): BO 6 (7, 8) sts, knit to end—58 (65, 68) sts.

Row 2 (WS): BO 6 (7, 8) sts, purl to end—52 (58, 60) sts.

Cont in St st and dec 1 st each side every other row 6 (6, 8) times—40 (46, 44) sts.

Size Small Only

Dec 1 st each side every row twice—36 sts.

Dec 1 st each side every other row 9 times—18 sts.

BO 2 sts at the beg of next 4 rows—10 sts.

BO rem 10 sts.

Sizes (Medium, Large) Only

Dec 1 st each side every other row (9, 8) times—(28, 28) sts.

Dec 1 st each side every 3rd row 2 times—(24, 24) sts.

BO 3 sts at beg of next 4 rows—(12, 12) sts.

BO rem 12 sts.

Left Sleeve

CO and work ribbing same as right sleeve for 2.5"/6.5cm.

Thumb Hole Opening

Rib 21 (25, 31) sts as est, drop yarn, join 2nd ball of yarn and BO 2 sts, work in est rib to end of row—29 (33, 39) sts.

Cont to follow right sleeve instructions to completion of sleeve.

Hood

Note: The hood is worked from front to back in 2 pieces each beg at front edge. The 2 pieces are later stitched tog then attached to body around neck opening. This hood fits extremely well because of the shaping.

Right Half

With smaller needles and A, CO 60 (62, 64) sts. Work in k1, p1 ribbing for 8 rows or 1"/2.5cm. Change to larger needles and St st. Work 4 rows even.

Beg Shaping

Row 1 (RS): Knit, dec 1 st each end of row—58 (60, 62) sts.

Row 2 (WS): Dec 1 st at beg of row (neck edge), purl to end—57 (59, 61) sts.

Place split ring marker at beg of WS row to mark neck edge.

Row 3: Knit to last 2 sts, k2tog (neck edge)—56 (58, 60) sts.

Rep Rows 2 and 3 twice more, then rep Row 2—51 (53, 55) sts.

Work even without decs for 10 rows.

Cont in St st, dec 1 st at neck edge every other row 4 times, AT THE SAME TIME, dec 1 st at opposite end (top of head) on 4th and 8th rows—45 (47, 49) sts.

Cont in St st for 16 rows, working even at neck edge; AT THE SAME TIME, dec 1 st at opposite edge (top of head) on 4th, 10th and 16th rows—42 (44, 46) sts.

Dec 1 st each side on next 9 (10, 11) rows—24 sts.

Next row: Work even.

Place rem 24 sts on holder for back of head.

Note: Piece should measure about 10 (10.25, 10.75)"/25.5 (26, 26.5)cm from front to back and about 15 (15.5, 16)"/38 (39.5, 40.5)cm from neck to top of head, measured at first 4 rows after ribbing.

Left Half

Work same as right half of hood to beg shaping.

Beg Shaping

Row 1 (RS): Knit, dec 1 st each end of row—58 (60, 62) sts.

Row 2 (WS): Purl, dec 1 st at end of row (neck edge)—57 (59, 61) sts.

Place split-ring marker into last st at end of WS row to mark neck edge.

Row 3: K2tog (neck edge), knit to end of row—56 (58, 60) sts.

Rep Rows 2 and 3 twice more, then rep Row 1—50 (52, 54) sts.

Work even for 10 rows.

Cont in St st, dec 1 st at neck edge every other row 4 times, AT THE SAME TIME, dec 1 st at opposite end (top of head) on 4th and 8th rows—44 (46, 48) sts.

Cont in St st for 16 rows, working even at neck edge; AT THE SAME TIME, dec 1 st at opposite edge (top of head) on the 4th, 8th, 12th, and 16th rows—40 (42, 44) sts.

Dec 1 st each side on next 8 (9, 10) rows—24 sts.

Next row: Work even.

Place rem 24 sts on holder.

Note: Piece should measure about 10 (10.25, 10.75)"/25.5 (26, 26.5)cm from front to back and about 15 (15.5, 16)"/38 (39.5, 40.5)cm from neck to top of head, measured at first 4 rows after ribbing.

Finishing

Weave in all ends. Block all pieces to size and air-dry.

Kangaroo Pocket

Place sweater front flat on table, RS facing and ribbing facing away from you. Thread tapestry needle with about 2 yds (2m) smooth cotton waste yarn in a light contrast color, thread the needle through each of the sts in the first row of St st above the last row of ribbing. (**Note:** This marker thread will help guide you when picking up sts in the same row for the pocket.) Place split ring marker after st 44 (after st 48, and in st 53) from side edge (the center of each size). Place one more marker 28 sts out from the center, place another marker 28 sts out from center on the other side—56 (56, 57) pocket sts. With smaller needles and A, pick up and p56 (56, 57) sts between markers. Change to larger needles and knit 1 row, inc 1 (1, 0) st—57 pocket sts. Purl next row. Beg with RS row, cont in St st foll Bird Chart for 19 rows, dec 1 st each side every 3rd row as shown—45 sts. Cont working pocket and beg on 2nd row after chart is finished, dec 1 st each side of pocket every other row 4 times—37 sts. Work 3 rows even. BO rem sts and steam pocket upward. Pin or baste BO edge to the sweater. With tapestry needle threaded with A, whipstitch the pocket to the sweater working neatly across BO edge.

Sweater

With WS facing out and tapestry needle threaded with A, sew shoulders tog using backstitch method and working close to shoulder edges to avoid bulky seams. Using backstitch, sew sleeves into armhole openings. Using mattress stitch, sew underarm seam from wrist to armpit and all the way down the side seam.

Hood

With WS together and tapestry needle threaded with A, using Kitchener st, graft the 24 sts from each holder tog at back of hood. Using mattress st, weave top of head and back of neck seams tog, taking care that edges meet neatly, especially at top of head where it will show. Baste or pin hood neck to sweater neck so that the hood center back seam matches the sweater center back and the hood front edges meet the neck opening edges. With WS facing out, backstitch hood around sweater neck, easing as necessary to fit both pieces tog.

Weave in ends, steam all seams. Air-dry completely.

Ties: Cut 6 strands of A about 30"/76cm in length. Braid the 6 strands tog, tying a knot in each end of braid to secure. Cut braid in half. With tapestry needle threaded with A, stitch one unknotted end of each braid onto the inside edge of neck opening where hood and center front meet. Stitch the other braid half at other edge of neck opening. Make 2 pom-poms and attach to braid ends.

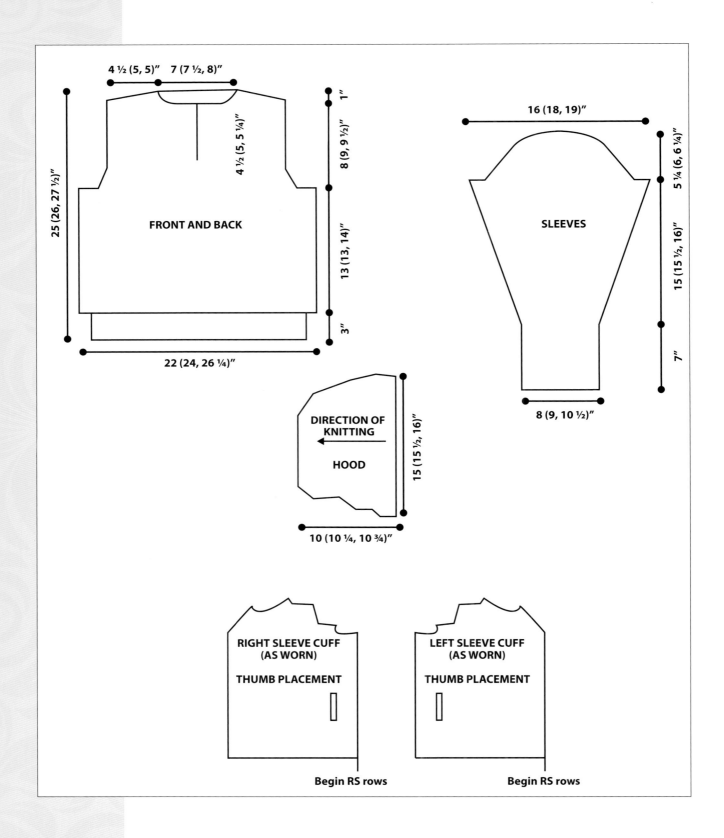

4 ½ (5, 5)"   7 (7 ½, 8)"

1"

8 (9, 9 ½)"

4 ½ (5, 5 ¼)"

25 (26, 27 ½)"

FRONT AND BACK

13 (13, 14)"

3"

22 (24, 26 ¼)"

16 (18, 19)"

SLEEVES

5 ¼ (6, 6 ¼)"

15 (15 ½, 16)"

7"

8 (9, 10 ½)"

DIRECTION OF
KNITTING

HOOD

15 (15 ½, 16)"

10 (10 ¼, 10 ¾)"

RIGHT SLEEVE CUFF
(AS WORN)

THUMB PLACEMENT

LEFT SLEEVE CUFF
(AS WORN)

THUMB PLACEMENT

Begin RS rows

Begin RS rows

Bird Chart

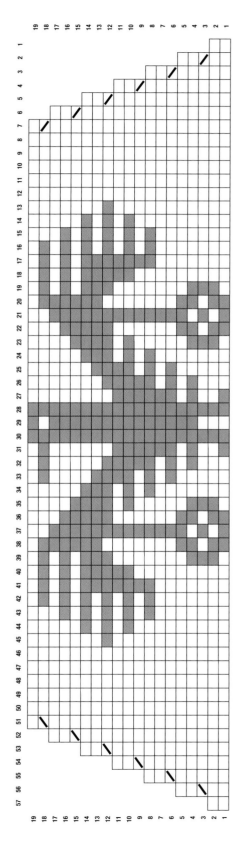

NORTHWEST FORGET-ME-NOT PULLOVER

DESIGN BY KRISTIN SPURKLAND

This sweater is inspired by my experiences camping, hiking, and boating in the western United States. When spending time in nature, warmth and comfort are of course very important, but it's also nice to feel like you look decent when going to a pub or a restaurant after finishing the adventure of the day. Forget Me Not features a pattern inspired by the western wildflowers; the color is reminiscent of my favorite wildflower, the forget-me-not. The optional mobius cowl offers both form and function: It keeps your neck warm when sitting around the campfire, while also showing off the texture of the wrong side of the pattern. ❧

Sizes
Woman's X-Small (**Small**, Medium, Large, X-Large)

Finished Measurements
Bust: 34 (**38**, 41.5, 45.5, 49.5, 53.5)"/86.5 (96.5, 105.5, 115.5, 125.5, 136)cm
Length: 21.5 (22, 23, 24.5, 25, 25.5)"/54.5 (56, 58.5, 62, 63.5, 65)cm

Materials (3)
◆ Louet *Gems Worsted*, 100% Merino wool; 100g/3.5oz; 175yds/160m per ball: Steel Grey #68, 8 (9, 10, 11, 12, 13) balls for the sweater; 2 additional balls for the cowl

◆ Size 9 (5.5mm) straight and 16"/40.5cm long circular needles or size needed to obtain gauge
◆ Size 5 (3.75) 16"/40.5 and 24"/61cm long circular needles
◆ Stitch holders or waste yarn
◆ Tapestry needle

Gauge
25 sts and 23 rows = 4"/10cm on larger needles in main pattern
Adjust needle size as necessary to obtain correct gauge.

PATTERN NOTES

The stitch pattern used for Forget Me Not must be worked on a needle larger than what is usually recommended for the yarn. Working on larger needles prevents the resulting fabric from being too dense and heavy.

The final (purl) row of each piece is worked on a smaller needle, to prevent the top edges from flaring.

STITCH PATTERN

Main Pattern (multiple of 4 + 3 sts):

Row 1: K2, (p3tog, knit same 3 sts tog, then purl same 3 sts tog, slip all 3 sts from needle, k1) across, end k1.

Rows 2 and 4: Purl.

Row 3: K4, (p3tog, knit same 3 sts tog, then purl same 3 sts tog, slip all 3 sts from needle, k1) across, end k3.

Rep Rows 1–4 for Main Pat.

INSTRUCTIONS

Back

With larger straight needles, CO 107 (119, 131, 143, 155, 167) sts.

Set-up row: K1, (p1, k1) across, working tbl (through back loop) of all sts.

Work in Main Pat until piece measures 14 (14, 14, 15, 15, 15)"/35.5 (35.5, 35.5, 38, 38, 38)cm from CO edge, ending after a WS row.

Armhole Shaping

Next row (RS): K1, ssk, work in pat to last 3 sts, k2tog, k1.

Next row (WS): Purl.

Rep these 2 rows 5 times more—95 (107, 119, 131, 143, 155) sts.

Work even in pat until piece measures 21.5 (22, 23, 24.5, 25, 25.5)"/54.5 (56, 58.5, 62, 63.5, 65)cm from CO edge, ending after a RS row. Change to smaller needle and work last WS row.

Shoulders and Neck

Place first 29 (33, 36, 41, 47, 53) sts on holder for right shoulder, place next 37 (41, 47, 49, 49, 49) sts on another holder for center back neck, place last 29 (33, 36, 41, 47, 53) sts on a 3rd holder for left shoulder.

Front

Work as for back until piece measures 14 (14, 14, 15, 15, 15)"/35.5 (35.5, 35.5, 38, 38, 38)cm from CO edge, ending after a WS row.

Armhole and Neck Shaping

Work same as back armhole shaping; at the same time, when piece measures 14.75 (14.5, 14.5, 15.5, 16, 16.5)"/37.5 (37, 37, 39.5, 40.5, 42) cm from CO edge, on a WS row, work to center st, place center st on holder, join 2nd ball of yarn, work to end.

Cont armhole shaping as est; at the same time, shape neck as foll:

RS: Work first side across to 3 sts from center front, k2tog, k1; then on 2nd side, k1, ssk, work to end.

WS: Purl.

Rep last 2 rows 17 (19, 22, 23, 23, 23) times more for neck decs—29 (33, 36, 41, 47, 53) sts rem at each shoulder.

Work even until same total length as back. Place shoulder sts on holders.

Sleeve

With larger straight needles, CO 51 (55, 59, 63, 67, 67) sts.

K1, (p1, k1) across, working tbl of all sts.

Work in Main Pat; at the same time, on Row 3 beg sleeve shaping as foll:

Inc row (RS): K2, M1, work in est pat to last 2 sts, M1, k2.

(WS): Work in est pat.

Rep inc row every foll 2nd row 0 (0, 7, 9, 11, 17) times more, then every 4th row 22 (22, 19, 18, 17, 14) times more, working inc sts into pat—97 (101, 113, 119, 125, 131) sts.

Work even until sleeve measures 17.5"/44.5cm or desired length, ending after a WS row.

Cap Shaping

RS: K1, ssk, work in pat to last 3 sts, k2tog, k1.

WS: Purl.

Rep last 2 rows 5 times more, ending after a RS row—85 (89, 101, 107, 113, 119) sts.

Change to smaller needles and work last WS row.

BO, knitting all sts tbl.

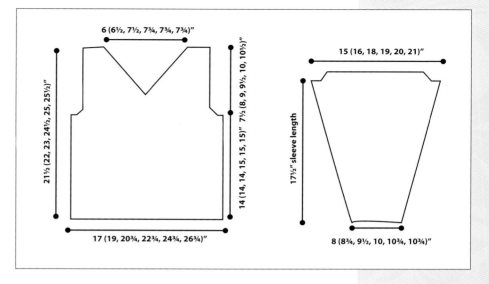

6 (6½, 7½, 7¾, 7¾, 7¾)"

21½ (22, 23, 24½, 25, 25½)"

14 (14, 14, 15, 15, 15)"

7½ (8, 9, 9½, 10, 10½)"

17 (19, 20¾, 22¾, 24¾, 26¾)"

15 (16, 18, 19, 20, 21)"

17½" sleeve length

8 (8¾, 9½, 10, 10¾, 10¾)"

Finishing

Join shoulders with 3-needle bind-off, using smaller needles.

Sew in sleeves. Sew sleeve and side seams. Weave in all ends.

Neckband

With RS facing, using smaller 16"/40.5cm circular needle and starting at right shoulder, pick up and knit 96 (106, 122, 126, 126, 126) sts around neck [29 (32, 37, 38, 38, 38) from each side of V-neck, 1 st from center front holder, 37 (41, 47, 49, 49, 49) sts from back holder]. Pm for beg of rnd and a split ring marker in center front st, join.

Next rnd: Knit to 1 st before marked center front st, slip 2 tog knitwise, k1, pass 2 slipped sts over knit st, knit to end of rnd.

Next rnd: Knit.

Rep last 2 rnds once more.

BO in knit.

Cowl

With larger circular needle, CO 229 sts. Do not join in-the-round.

Set up row: P1, (k1, p1) to end working tbl of all sts. Do not turn work at end of row.

Join and work in-the-round, *twisting sts over the needle one time*, so that the scarf will create a Möbius. Pm for beg of rnd.

Rnd 1: K1, (k1, p3tog, knit same 3 sts tog, then purl same 3 sts tog, slip all 3 sts from needle) around.

Rnds 2 and 4: Knit.

Rnd 3: (P3tog, knit same 3 sts tog, then purl same 3 sts tog, slip all 3 sts from needle, k1) around, end k1.

Rep Rnds 1–4 until cowl measures 5.5"/14cm, ending after Rnd 1 or Rnd 3.

Change to smaller needle and work final Row 2 or Row 4.

BO, knitting all sts tbl.

Weave in all ends.

ABBREVIATIONS

beg	begin(s), beginning		psso	pass slip st(s) over
BO	bind off		pwise	purlwise (as if to purl)
CC	contrast color		rem	remain(s), remaining
cm	centimeter(s)		rep(s)	repeat(s), repeated, repeating
CO	cast on		rnd(s)	round(s)
cont	continue, continuing		RH	right-hand
dec(s)	decrease, decreasing, decreases		RS	right side (of work)
dpn	double-pointed needle(s)		revsc	reverse single crochet (crab st)
est	establish, established		sc	single crochet
foll	follow(s), following		sl	slip, slipped, slipping
inc(s)	increase(s), increasing		sm	slip marker
k	knit		ssk	[slip 1 st knitwise] twice from left needle to right needle, insert left needle tip into fronts of both slipped sts, knit both sts together from this position (decrease)
k1f&b	knit into front then back of same st (increase)			
k1f,b,&f	knitting into front, back, then front again of same st (increase 2 sts)			
k1-tbl	knit 1 st through back loop		ssp	[slip 1 st knitwise] twice from left needle to right needle, return both sts to left needle and purl both together through back loops
k2tog	knit 2 sts together (decrease)			
k2tog-tbl	knit 2 sts together through back loops			
kwise	knitwise (as if to knit)		st(s)	stitch(es)
LH	left-hand		St st	stockinette stitch
m(s)	marker(s)		tbl	through back loop
MC	main color		tog	together
mm	millimeter(s)		w&t	wrap next stitch, then turn work (often used in short rows)
M1	make 1 (increase)			
M1k	make 1 knitwise		WS	wrong side (of work)
M1p	make 1 purlwise		wyib	with yarn in back
pat(s)	pattern(s)		wyif	with yarn in front
p	purl		yb	yarn back
p1f&b	purl into front then back of same st (increase)		yf	yarn forward
p1-tbl	purl 1 st through back loop		yo	yarn over
p2tog	purl 2 sts together (decrease)		*	repeat instructions from *
pm	place marker		( )	alternate measurements and/or instructions
			[ ]	instructions to be worked as a group a specified number of times

YARN SOURCES

Berroco
www.berroco.com

Blue Sky Alpacas
www.blueskyalpacas.com

Brown Sheep
www.brownsheep.com

Cascade Yarns
www.cascadeyarns.com

Elemental Affects
www.elementalaffects.com

Finullgarn
www.nordicfiberarts.com

ístex
www.istex.is

Jamieson & Smith
www.shetlandwoolbrokers.co.uk

Lana Grossa
www.lanagrossa.com

Louet
www.louet.com

Muench Yarns
www.muenchyarns.com

Reynolds Yarns
www.jcacrafts.com

Rowan
www.rowanyarns.co.uk

Schoolhouse Press
www.schoolhousepress.com

Westminster Fibers
www.westminsterfibers.com

STANDARD YARN WEIGHT SYSTEM

Categories of yarn, gauge ranges, and recommended needle and hook sizes

Yarn Weight Symbol & Category Names	0 Lace	1 Super Fine	2 Fine	3 Light	4 Medium	5 Bulky	6 Super Bulky
Type of Yarns in Category	Fingering 10 count crochet thread	Sock, Fingering, Baby	Sport, Baby	DK, Light Worsted	Worsted, Afghan, Aran	Chunky, Craft, Rug	Bulky, Roving
Knit Gauge Range* in Stockinette Stitch to 4 inches	33–40** sts	27–32 sts	23–26 sts	21–24 sts	16–20 sts	12–15 sts	6–11 sts
Recommended Needle in Metric Size Range	1.5–2.25 mm	2.25–3.25 mm	3.25–3.75 mm	3.75–4.5 mm	4.5–5.5 mm	5.5–8 mm	8mm and larger
Recommended Needle U.S. Size Range	000 to 1	1 to 3	3 to 5	5 to 7	7 to 9	9 to 11	11 and larger
Crochet Gauge* Ranges in Signle Crochet to 4 inch	32–42 double crochets**	21–31 sts	16–20 sts	12–17 sts	11–14 sts	8–11 sts	5–9 sts
Recommended Hook in Metric Size Range	Steel*** 1.6–1.4mm Regular hook 2.25mm	2.25–3.5 mm	3.5–4.5 mm	4.5–5.5 mm	5.5–6.5 mm	6.5–9 mm	9mm and larger
Recommended Hook U.S. Size Range	Steel*** 6, 7, 8 Regular hook B–1	B–1 to E–4	E–4 to 7	7 to I–9	I–9 to K–10 ½	K–10 ½ to M–13	M–13 and larger

* GUIDELINES ONLY: The above reflect the most commonly used gauges and needle or hook sizes for specific yarn categories.

** Lace weight yarns are usually knitted or crocheted on larger needles and hooks to create lacy, openwork patterns. Accordingly, a gauge range is difficult to determine. Always follow the gauge stated in your pattern.

*** Steel crochet hooks are sized differently from regular hooks—the higher the number, the smaller the hook, which is reverse of regular hook sizing.

This Standards & Guidelines booklet and downloadable symbol artwork are available at: **YarnStandards.com**.

ABOUT THE DESIGNERS

Dawn Brocco began her designing career working freelance for most of the major knitting publications. She has been self-publishing for the past thirteen years and now has more than one hundred patterns available. Her style embraces classic design with modern twists and whimsical design based on a love of nature. You can find Dawn Brocco Knitwear Designs at www.dawnbrocco.com, and you can reach Dawn at dawn@dawnbrocco.com.

Beth Brown-Reinsel has been teaching knitting workshops nationally, as well as internationally, for more than twenty years. She wrote the book *Knitting Ganseys* and has recently filmed the DVD *Knitting Ganseys with Beth Brown-Reinsel*. Her articles have appeared in *Threads*; *Cast On*; *Interweave Knits*; *Shuttle, Spindle, Dye Pot*; *Vogue Knitting*; *and Knitter's* magazines. She continues to design for her own pattern line, available at www.knittingtraditions.com. Beth lives happily in Vermont.

Donna Druchunas is the author of numerous books, including *Successful Lace Knitting: Celebrating the Work of Dorothy Reade*, *Ethnic Knitting Exploration: Lithuania, Iceland, and Ireland*, and *Arctic Lace: Knitted Projects and Stories Inspired by Alaska's Native Knitters*. She spent four months this year traveling in Europe to teach knitting workshops and do research for her next book, which will be about knitting in Lithuania. Visit her website at www.sheeptoshawl.com.

Sue Flanders has been designing knitwear for more than twenty years. Her patterns have appeared in many publications, including *Interweave Knits, Knitter's*, and *Cast-On* magazines and in two books by Melanie Falick, *Knitting in America* and *Kids Knitting*. She is coauthor of *Norwegian Handknits: Heirloom Designs from Vesterheim Museum* (Voyageur Press, 2009) and *Swedish Handknits: A Collection of Heirloom Designs* (Voyageur Press, 2012).

Gretchen Funk lives and knits in Minnesota, where she and her husband own and operate the Triple Rock Social Club. She teaches knitting at The Yarnery in St. Paul and Crafty Planet, a needlework and craft shop in Minneapolis.

Kate Larson loves using fiber arts as a bridge between her passions for art and agriculture. Her fiber journey has led her to a year of study in England, a degree in environmental soil chemistry, a tour of Estonian textile traditions, and back to the farm where her family has lived for six generations. She keeps an ever-growing flock of Border Leicester sheep and teaches handspinning and knitting regularly in central Indiana and around the country. Kate has published articles and designs in *Spin-Off* magazine and is a regular contributor to the Spinner's Connection blog at SpinningDaily.com. You can find her at KateLarsonTextiles.com.

A prolific designer, **Melissa Leapman** is the author of several bestselling knitting and crocheting books. Recent titles are *Hot Knits* and *Cool Crochet* (Watson-Guptill, 2004 and 2005), as well as the popular *Cables Untangled* and *Continuous Cables* (Potter Craft, 2006 and 2008). Her newest releases, *Color Knitting the Easy Way* and *Mastering Color Knitting*, were published in 2010. The must-have *Stash Buster Knits* was published in Fall 2011, also by Potter Craft.

Hélène Magnússon is best known for her research around the traditional Icelandic intarsia that was seen in knitted inserts in shoes in Iceland in the past centuries. Her book, *Icelandic Knitting: Using Rose Patterns*, is available in three languages. She is a French native but a true Icelandic knitter and has an Icelandic family. Find out more about her on her website: www.helenemagnusson.com.

Heather Ordover's latest joy has been writing and editing the first pattern book in the series *What Would Madame Defarge Knit? Creations Inspired by Classic Characters* . Prior to that, she spent her time writing and recording essays for *Cast-On: A Podcast for Knitters* and currently hosts her own long-running podcast, *CraftLit: A Podcast for Crafters Who Love Books* (think "audiobook with benefits"). Her crafty writing has appeared in *Spin-Off*, *WeaveZine*, and *The Arizona Daily Star*.

Cynthia LeCount Samaké is a specialist in indigenous textiles and festival costume. Decades ago, while traveling overland through South America, she was enthralled with the fine, intricately patterned knitting from Peru and Bolivia. She collected a dozen hand-knit caps from different regions, then attempted to research Andean knitting once she arrived home. But nothing had been written on the subject, so she began annual forays to research, photograph, and collect knitted examples. The result of this study was her book *Andean Folk Knitting: Traditions and Techniques from Peru and Bolivia*, published in 1990 and now out of print. Later, Cynthia began Behind the Scenes Adventures, leading groups on textile and festival tours. In 2000, her Malian

husband, Barou, joined her in the business, and they added numerous destinations to the trip calendar. She has traveled to Peru and Bolivia over forty times and never tires of seeing Machu Picchu! See Cynthia's TEXTILE TOUR website for Behind the Scenes Adventures at www.btsadventures.com.

Kristin Spurkland learned to knit from her roommate, Sophie, in her freshman year of college. In 1998, she received her degree in apparel design from Bassist College in Portland, Oregon, and decided to pursue a career in knitwear design. She has been designing ever since. Kristin is the author of four books, including *The Knitting Man(ual)*, Ten Speed Press, 2007.

Candace Eisner Strick has immersed herself in music and knitting most of her life. Now retired from sixteen years of

teaching cello, she concentrates on designing, writing, and teaching knitting. She is the author many knitting pattern books, has been published in numerous magazines, and has taught nationally and internationally since 1998. She is the creator of her own line of yarn, Merging Colors, and her own line of patterns under the name of Strickwear (www.strickwear.com). You can read her blog at www.candaceeisnerstrickknitting.blogspot.com.

Pinpilan Wangsai taught herself to knit from library books while living in Bangkok. People thought she was crazy for knitting scarves and hats in the constant heat. Three years later, she is living in Tokyo where she is delighted to find that there are four seasons a year, and she can now knit and wear something bigger than a bikini without having a heat stroke. Read about her craft ventures at http://www.getcrafty.com/blogs.php?user=dumplingrrl.

INDEX